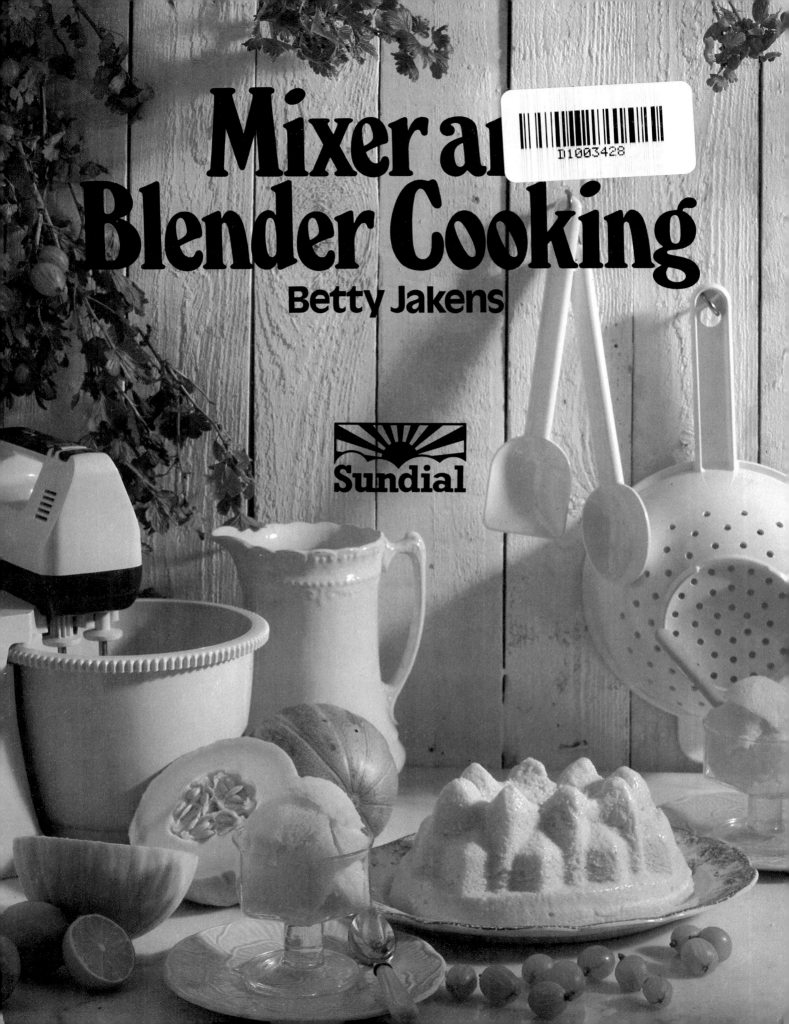

Mixer and Blender Cooking

Betty Jakens

Sundial

Contents

First published in 1981 by Octopus Books Limited
59 Grosvenor Street, London W1

Second impression, 1981

© 1981 Hennerwood Publications Limited

ISBN 0 906320 22 4

Printed in England by Severn Valley Press Limited

INTRODUCTION

When you invest in a mixer or blender you rediscover the fun of cooking. With all the long, laborious, arm-aching jobs, which once had to be done by hand now taken care of by the flick of a switch, there is more time to experiment with many new recipes.

There is great satisfaction in presenting the family or guests with home-prepared dishes, which previously you may have bought ready-made. It's even better when your efforts win you compliments. Pâtés, soups, unusual salad dressings and sauces, puddings flavoured with fresh fruit purée or made with meringue – these are just a few of the dishes which take less effort and time to make with the aid of a mixer or blender.

In order to get the maximum use and best results from a mixer or blender you need to understand the jobs they can perform as well as their limitations. The information and recipes in this book will give you a good idea of the different food preparation methods and jobs for which mixers and blenders can be used.

General guide

Hand mixer: this type of mixer has twin beaters and an ejector button to release them after use. One, two or three speed models are available. A wall bracket for storage is usually supplied. A stand and bowl attachment is often available as an optional extra. The usual bowl capacity is up to 1 kg/2¼ lb total cake weight.

Hand mixers are portable and do not require a specially designed mixing bowl if hand-held. They cannot cope with stiff mixtures such as bread doughs or rich fruit cakes.

Hand mixer and blender: this hand mixer, usually with three speeds, has an outlet from the mixer motor to drive a small blender. The goblet usually has a scant 1 pint/500 ml capacity. A wall bracket for storage is supplied with some models.

Hand mixer with stand, bowl and blender: some of the more powerful hand mixers have dough kneading hooks included as an attachment. The usual bowl capacity is up to 1 kg/2¼ lb total cake weight. On some models a mincer and a slicer and shredder can be added as optional extras.

Table mixer: a table mixer cannot be used as a portable mixer. It is a larger, more sophisticated version of the mixer, stand and bowl combination with a greater speed variation. This type of mixer copes with larger quantities: the mixing bowl can take up to a 3 kg/6 lb cake mixture and kneads a

750 g/1½ lb bread dough. A number of attachments such as a blender, mincer, slicer and shredder, potato peeler, juice extractor and can opener can be operated from the basic mixer.

Blender: a motor unit houses the blender. The goblet capacity is usually either a scant 600 ml or 1 litre/1 pint or 1¾ pints. Some goblets can be taken apart for cleaning. There is usually one operating speed, but some large capacity blenders have a speed selection. Coffee mill attachments are supplied with some blenders.

Food processor: the latest type of food preparation machine, which is very quick and most jobs are performed in seconds. Mixing, blending and chopping are carried out in the same bowl which has a central metal cutting blade. A plastic blade, used for some mixing jobs, is usually supplied as well.

The bowl and centrally positioned blade fit on top of a powerful motor unit and are covered by a lid with a hopper. Cutting discs for slicing and shredding vegetables and salads fit on to the central drive and are supplied with the machine.

Some recipes require new preparation techniques, but many methods are similar to those used in a blender. A greater quantity of ingredients can be processed at one time.

From the front, clockwise: Hand mixer; Blender; Table mixer

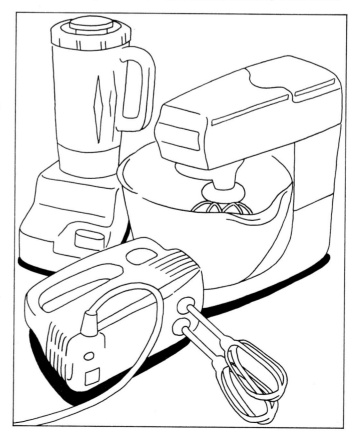

Using the appliance

It is advisable to check with the manufacturer's instruction manual to ensure that the jobs listed below are suitable for your mixer or blender.

Mixers can be used for
- creaming fat and sugar and beating in the eggs for cakes and puddings. Table mixers and some of the more powerful hand mixers on stands with speed variations can be used to fold in flour and fruit to a creamed fat, sugar and egg mixture.
- rubbing fat into flour for shortcrust and flan pastries, scones and plain cakes. Table mixers and some of the more powerful hand mixers with speed variations can be used to mix in the water.
- whisking eggs and sugar for sponge cakes, cold soufflés and mousses. Hand mixers are perfect for whisking over hot water.
- whisking egg whites for meringues, mousses and soufflés.
- beating the eggs into the cooked panada for choux pastry.
- whisking batters for pancakes, fritters and batter puddings.
- mixing and kneading yeasted doughs (if a special dough hook is supplied for the mixer).
- whipping cream.
- making mayonnaise.
- mixing and beating icings.
- making ice cream.
- creaming cooked potatoes, mashing swedes and celeriac.

Blenders can be used for
- puréeing cooked vegetables such as spinach.
- puréeing cooked vegetables in stock to make soup. Small amounts of cooked meat can be added.
- puréeing cooked fruit for sauces and flavouring puddings. Add more or less liquid (fruit juice, sugar syrup or water) to adjust the consistency.
- making 'juicy' raw fruits such as tomatoes, strawberries, raspberries and other soft fruits into purées without the addition of water. To remove the pips or seeds pass the purée through a fine nylon sieve. Use for sauces, puddings and ice cream.
- making breadcrumbs from fresh or stale bread. Fresh herbs (well dried) can be added with the bread to chop them for stuffings.
- making oven-dried bread into raspings (golden breadcrumbs) for coating meat and fish.
- making biscuit crumbs for flan cases and puddings.
- making pâtés, spreads and dips. Use cooked meats, liver and vegetables and add a small quantity of liquid, melted butter, lemon juice, cream etc. to make a smooth mixture.
- blending sauces.

- making mayonnaise and salad dressings.
- blending drinks (milk shakes, fruit drinks, cocktails).
- puréeing baby foods.
- blending batters for pancakes, fritters and batter puddings.
- chopping fresh herbs. These are usually best chopped in liquid from the recipe, e.g. stock or milk for soups and sauces, oil and vinegar, or mayonnaise, for salad dressings, raw egg for stuffings.
- chopping hard raw vegetables for salads and soups.
- chopping firm and hard cheese (Cheddar, Parmesan).
- chopping and grinding nuts.
- making powdered sugar from granulated sugar (looks like icing sugar).
- grinding coffee beans (not recommended for all blenders).
- crushing ice.

Note: most small and some larger blenders do not cope with chopping hard foods such as ice cubes, cheese, raw vegetables, nuts and coffee beans.

How to get the best from your mixer or blender

For maximum use, both mixers and blenders should be kept out on, or near to, the food preparation area. Machines stored away in a cupboard are not regularly used because it seems 'too much effort' to get them out for the one preparation job.

Read carefully the manufacturer's instruction manual, and recipe booklet if one is supplied, for assembling and operating instructions, minimum and maximum quantities, the types of food which can be prepared with the mixer and in the blender and the maximum mixing and blending operating times. Do not try to prepare more than the recommended maximum quantity as overloading can cause damage to the motor, and the ingredients will either spill over from the mixing bowl or blender goblet or not be effectively prepared.

Hand mixers are more efficient if at least half of the working end of the beaters is covered by the mixture. So try to use the correct-sized mixing bowl for the job in hand. Deep bowls with straight sides are best, but generally any rigid mixing bowl can be used.

Save time and washing up by planning food preparation jobs ahead to prevent unnecessary repetition of a particular job over a 2 or 3 day period. For instance, if you are planning to serve shortcrust pastry in several savoury and sweet recipes over the next few days, make the total quantity of pastry dough required for all the recipes or the maximum quantity the mixer will take at one time. To calculate the amount of prepared dough required, add together the total weight of the ingredients that would be used to make the dough for a particular recipe and weigh off that amount from the bulk quantity. For example, for dough made from 200 g/8 oz flour and 100 g/4 oz fat, weigh off approximately 350 g/12 oz prepared dough. Wrap unused dough in cling film or foil and store in the refrigerator for up to 3–4 days.

With a mixer it does not take longer to prepare larger quantities of creamed sponge cake mixtures, so it is a good idea either to duplicate the recipe and freeze one of the cakes, or to make part of the mixture into another cake variety or a steamed or baked sponge pudding.

Similar advance planning can be applied to using the blender for making breadcrumbs and fruit purées, which freeze well, and mayonnaise which can be stored in the refrigerator.

Mixer tips

Creaming fat and sugar
Ensure that the fat and eggs are at the same room temperature; take them out of the refrigerator about 2 hours before required. Hard fat is difficult to cream and cold eggs added to creamed fat and sugar often causes the mixture to curdle.

Warming the mixing bowls and beaters helps to prevent the fat sticking to the sides of the bowl or to the beaters. Pour warm, not hot, water into the bowl, place the beaters in it and leave for a few minutes. Dry thoroughly. If the bowl is too hot the fat will melt when placed in the bowl.

It should not take longer than 3 minutes to beat fat and sugar to a light creamy consistency, 20–30 seconds to beat in each egg and less than 20 seconds to fold in flour. If you have a telephone call, or other interruption, switch off the mixer.

Rubbing fat into flour
Use room temperature fat which is at a 'just spreadable' consistency. Both hard and soft fat are difficult to rub in evenly; hard fat tends to fly out of the mixing bowl and very soft fat gives a difficult to handle dough and crumbly baked results.

Be careful not to over-rub the fat into the flour. The rubbed-in mixture should resemble fine breadcrumbs. If it begins to stick together, it has been mixed for too long. Switch off immediately rubbing-in is completed.

If the mixer is used to mix in the water, switch on the mixer and add the measured water quickly to ensure it is evenly mixed in. Switch off immediately the dough is formed.

Folding in flour
Flour can be folded in by the mixer, but first check with the manufacturer's instructions. Mixers without a speed variation should not be used for folding in as a low speed is required for this job. Once the flour is incorporated, switch off the mixer.

Making bread
Bread can only be made with mixers which have special dough mixing attachments. Follow the manufacturer's instructions for quantity and kneading time.

Egg whites
The smallest trace of grease will prevent egg whites from forming a stiff foam, so always make sure that the bowl and beaters are grease-free. Check your hands, too, before separating eggs. It is preferable to use egg whites at room temperature as they whisk up more quickly and give a larger volume. There are two degrees of stiffness for whisking egg whites depending on how they are to be used. For soufflés and mousses, whisk the whites until just stiff, or until they stand in soft peaks; when the beaters are withdrawn from the whites the peaks should just fall over at the top. The whites should look 'shiny' in appearance. If the whites are too stiff they will be difficult to fold into the other mixture and little islands of whisked white will be left. For meringues, the whites must be whisked until very stiff, i.e. until they stand in stiff straight peaks when the beaters are lifted out of the whites. The whites should be 'dull' in appearance. If they are insufficiently whisked when the sugar is added, a marshmallow consistency will result which gives poor meringues and a smaller volume.

Blender tips

Do not under- or over-fill the goblet. The blades should always be covered by food. As a general guide, for dry and semi-liquid foods, the goblet should not be more than about one-third full; for liquid ingredients it can be almost full, but remember to leave about 5 cm/2 inches head-room to allow for the movement of the ingredients when the blender is switched on.

Always allow the food to cool slightly before placing it in the goblet. Boiling or very hot food or liquid may damage or break the goblet and also makes it difficult to handle when placing the blender goblet on the motor unit.

When preparing several types of food for a particular recipe, always prepare the dry ingredients first to avoid washing and drying the goblet between the various stages.

Breadcrumbs

Breadcrumbs can be made from fresh or stale bread. In most blenders soft crusts can be crumbed as well, if wished.

To make breadcrumbs in the blender, cut or break the bread into pieces small enough to go through the hole in the centre of the lid. Switch on the motor and drop the bread pieces through the centre of the lid on to the revolving blades. Do not fill the goblet more than one-third full. Repeat until sufficient breadcrumbs are made.

Fresh herbs can be added to the bread to chop them at the same time. Ensure that they are thoroughly dried after washing though.

Powdered sugar

Granulated sugar can be ground to a fine caster sugar or icing sugar consistency in the blender. It can be used for cake-making, butter icing (not other icings as it will not set), drinks or for sprinkling on pies and fruit. Do not fill the goblet more than one-third full at a time.

Cleaning

Motor unit: remove the plug from the socket before cleaning. Wipe the surface with a soft damp cloth, using a little washing-up liquid if necessary. Dry with a soft cloth. Do not use abrasive cleaners.

Mixing bowl and beaters: wash in the usual way.

Blender: rinse the goblet in warm running water. For strong flavoured, greasy and sticky ingredients half fill the goblet with warm water, cover with the lid and switch on for a few seconds. Add one drop of detergent if necessary. Rinse well and drain or dry thoroughly.

Safety notes

Check that the correct amp fuse for the motor wattage is fitted to fused plugs.

Always switch off and unplug machines after use, especially if young children are in the house.

For hand-held mixers, use the nearest electrical point to avoid tripping over flexes. At the cooker be careful not to let the flex trail over the hob to prevent it from being damaged by the heat. Always switch off the motor before lifting the beaters from the mixing bowl.

For blenders, always switch off the motor before removing the lid from the goblet. Do not place boiling or very hot food or liquid in the blender goblet. It may crack or damage the goblet.

Recipe note

The following symbols indicate which type of machine can be used for each recipe:

Table mixer   Hand mixer   Blender   Table or hand mixer

STARTERS

Home-made soups make a popular, inexpensive first course, and a blender eliminates the dreary task of hand sieving, making a finely chopped or creamy puréed soup in seconds. Blender-made soups rarely need to be thickened, especially if potatoes or other root vegetables are included in the ingredients. If extra thickening is required, a little instant potato or flour can be added to the soup in the blender and mixed in for a few seconds.

For the preparation of large quantities of soup, purée the cooked vegetables and stock in batches using roughly equal amounts of vegetable and stock for each batch. Fresh herbs are quickly chopped when added to soups, sauces or dressings in the blender.

Smooth pâtés made from cooked fish, liver and meat are simple to prepare in the blender to make a more substantial starter. It may be necessary to switch off the blender from time to time and to scrape down the mixture on to the blender blades and then continue to blend until it becomes smooth.

Other starter ideas are given in the Sauces and Salad Dressings chapter on pages 34–43.

Lemon and chiken soup

Metric	Imperial
25 g butter	*1 oz butter*
1 medium onion, peeled and chopped	*1 medium onion, peeled and chopped*
750 ml chicken stock	*1¼ pints chicken stock*
100 g cooked chicken or turkey meat, roughly chopped	*4 oz cooked chicken or turkey meat, roughly chopped*
1 × 15 ml spoon cornflour	*1 tablespoon cornflour*
3 × 15 ml spoons lemon juice	*3 tablespoons lemon juice*
1 × 2.5 ml spoon salt	*½ teaspoon salt*
white pepper	*white pepper*
150 ml double cream	*¼ pint double cream*
2 egg yolks	*2 egg yolks*
chopped chives or fresh parsley, to garnish	*chopped chives or fresh parsley, to garnish*

Preparation time: 15 minutes
Cooking time: about 15 minutes

Melt the butter in a large pan, add the onion and cook over a low heat for about 10 minutes until the onion is soft and transparent.

Place the onion, stock and cooked chicken in the blender goblet and add the cornflour. Blend until smooth. Return to the pan and bring to the boil, stirring. Stir in the lemon juice, salt and pepper. Finally add the cream. Cool slightly.

Mix a little of the soup with the egg yolks and add to the pan, stirring continuously. Do not allow to boil or the egg yolks will curdle. Serve immediately with chopped chives or parsley sprinkled on top.

Serves 4–6

Gazpacho

Metric

450 g ripe tomatoes,
    roughly chopped
1 garlic clove, peeled
1 large onion, preferably
    Spanish, peeled
1 large green pepper,
    cored and seeded
½ large cucumber, peeled
1 slice white bread, cut
    1 cm thick, crusts
    removed
3 × 15 ml spoons salad oil
2–3 × 15 ml spoons lemon
    juice
salt
cayenne pepper
1 × 550 ml can tomato
    juice, chilled

To serve:

2 ripe tomatoes, skinned,
    seeded and finely
    chopped
croûtons

Imperial

1 lb ripe tomatoes,
    roughly chopped
1 garlic clove, peeled
1 large onion, preferably
    Spanish, peeled
1 large green pepper,
    cored and seeded
½ large cucumber, peeled
1 slice white bread, cut
    ½ inch thick, crusts
    removed
3 tablespoons salad oil
2–3 tablespoons lemon
    juice
salt
cayenne pepper
1 × 19 fl oz can tomato
    juice, chilled

To serve:

2 ripe tomatoes, skinned,
    seeded and finely
    chopped
croûtons

Preparation time: 15 minutes (excluding chilling time)

Place the tomatoes and garlic clove in the blender goblet. Blend until the tomatoes are puréed.
Roughly chop half of the onion, green pepper and cucumber and add to the tomatoes in the goblet. Break the bread into small pieces and add to the goblet. Blend until the vegetables are finely chopped. If the goblet is too small to take all the ingredients in one batch, add a proportion of each ingredient in each quantity to be blended.
Strain the purée to remove the tomato seeds and skin. Chill in a covered bowl for at least 6 hours.
Blend together the salad oil, lemon juice and salt and cayenne to taste. Add the purée mixture with the tomato juice and mix well. Adjust the seasoning. Chill in the refrigerator.
To serve, finely chop the remaining onion, green pepper and cucumber. Place the chopped vegetables including the tomatoes, and the croûtons in individual dishes and the soup in a tureen or in soup bowls. Hand the chopped vegetables and croûtons separately.
Serves 4–6

Lemon and chicken soup; Gazpacho

Brussels sprout soup

Preparation time: 15 minutes
Cooking time: about 20 minutes

Metric
15 g butter
1 large onion, peeled
  and chopped
900 ml chicken stock
1 large potato, peeled
  and cut into 6
450 g Brussels sprouts,
  trimmed
salt
freshly ground black
  pepper
large pinch of ground
  nutmeg
6 × 15 ml spoons double
  cream

Imperial
½ oz butter
1 large onion, peeled
  and chopped
1½ pints chicken stock
1 large potato, peeled
  and cut into 6
1 lb Brussels sprouts,
  trimmed
salt
freshly ground black
  pepper
large pinch of ground
  nutmeg
6 tablespoons double
  cream

Melt the butter in a large pan, add the onion and cook over a low heat for 5 minutes. Add the stock and potato and bring to the boil. Cover and simmer for 10 minutes.

Add the Brussels sprouts, salt, pepper and nutmeg, bring back to the boil and cook for 8–10 minutes or until just cooked. Be careful not to overcook the sprouts or the flavour will be spoilt. Leave the mixture to cool slightly.

Place the vegetables and stock in the blender goblet and blend until smooth. Reheat and adjust the seasoning. Stir in the cream just before serving.

Serves 6

Curried carrot soup with creamed apple

Metric	Imperial
25 g butter	1 oz butter
2 medium onions, peeled and roughly chopped	2 medium onions, peeled and roughly chopped
2 × 5 ml spoons mild curry powder	2 teaspoons mild curry powder
450 g carrots, peeled and coarsely chopped	1 lb carrots, peeled and coarsely chopped
1 thick lemon slice, pipped	1 thick lemon slice, pipped
1.2 litres chicken stock	2 pints chicken stock
salt	salt
freshly ground black pepper	freshly ground black pepper

For the creamed apple:

Metric	Imperial
450 g cooking apples, peeled, cored and thickly sliced	1 lb cooking apples, peeled, cored and thickly sliced
1 × 15 ml spoon sugar	1 tablespoon sugar
5 × 15 ml spoons water	5 tablespoons water
5 × 15 ml spoons double cream	5 tablespoons double cream

Preparation time: 15 minutes
Cooking time: about 40 minutes

Melt the butter in a large saucepan, add the onions and cook over a low heat for 5 minutes. Stir in the curry powder and cook for 3 minutes. Add all the remaining ingredients, with salt and pepper to taste. Bring to the boil, then reduce the heat, cover the pan and simmer for 30 minutes or until the chopped carrots are soft.

Meanwhile, to make the creamed apple, place the apples, sugar and water in a medium saucepan, cover and cook for about 10 minutes or until soft. Cool slightly. Place in the blender goblet and blend until puréed. Leave to cool completely. Using a hand mixer, half whip the cream. Fold into the apple purée.

Cool the soup slightly, then place in the blender goblet and blend until puréed. Return to the pan and reheat. Adjust the seasoning.

Serve the carrot soup piping hot and hand the creamed apple separately.

Serves 6

Green pea and bacon soup

Metric	Imperial
15 g butter	½ oz butter
1 medium onion, peeled and chopped	1 medium onion, peeled and chopped
1 rasher streaky bacon, rind removed, chopped	1 rasher streaky bacon, rind removed, chopped
900 ml chicken stock	1½ pints chicken stock
1 medium potato, peeled and cut into 4	1 medium potato, peeled and cut into 4
450 g frozen peas	1 lb frozen peas
salt	salt
freshly ground black pepper	freshly ground black pepper

Bacon croûtons:

Metric	Imperial
3 × 1 cm thick slices white or brown bread, crusts removed	3 × ½ inch thick slices white or brown bread, crusts removed
3 × 15 ml spoons cooking oil	3 tablespoons cooking oil
2 rashers streaky bacon, rind removed, finely chopped	2 rashers streaky bacon, rind removed, finely chopped

Preparation time: 10 minutes
Cooking time: about 30 minutes

Melt the butter in a large pan, add the onion and streaky bacon and cook over a low heat for 5 minutes. Add the chicken stock and potato, bring to the boil, cover and simmer for 10 minutes.

Add the peas, salt and pepper and cook for a further 10–15 minutes. Leave to cool slightly.

Place the vegetables and stock in the blender goblet and blend until smooth. Reheat and check the seasoning.

To make the bacon croûtons, cut the bread slices into 1 cm/½ inch cubes. Heat 1 × 15 ml spoon/1 tablespoon of the oil in a large frying pan, add the bacon and cook over a moderate heat until crisp. Remove from the pan. Heat the remaining oil in the pan, add the bread cubes and fry until evenly browned and crisp. Return the bacon to the pan and toss with the bread cubes.

To serve, hand the bacon croûtons separately at the table with the hot soup.

Serves 4–6

From the back, clockwise: Green pea and bacon soup; Creamed apple; Curried carrot soup; Brussels sprout soup

Soup of the earth

Preparation time: about 15 minutes
Cooking time: about 30 minutes

Metric
25 g butter
1 large onion, peeled and
    chopped
100 g potatoes, peeled
    and roughly chopped
225 g carrots, peeled and
    thickly sliced
225 g swede, peeled and
    roughly chopped
900 ml chicken stock
small bunch of parsley
300 ml milk
salt
freshly ground black
    pepper

Imperial
1 oz butter
1 large onion, peeled and
    chopped
4 oz potatoes, peeled and
    roughly chopped
8 oz carrots, peeled and
    thickly sliced
8 oz swede, peeled and
    roughly chopped
1½ pints chicken stock
small bunch of parsley
½ pint milk
salt
freshly ground black
    pepper

Melt the butter in a large saucepan, add the onion and fry gently until soft. Add all the other ingredients, except the parsley, milk, salt and pepper, and bring to the boil. Cover the pan and simmer until the vegetables are soft. Leave to cool slightly.

Place the vegetables, stock and parsley in the blender goblet and blend until the parsley is chopped and the vegetables are smooth. Return to the pan, add the milk and reheat. Adjust the seasoning. Serve with hot French bread.

Serves 6–8

From the left: Soup of the earth; Lentil potage; Fresh tomato soup

Lentil potage

Metric
450 g ham knuckle, soaked
    overnight
175 g red lentils
1 large onion, peeled
    and chopped
1 medium carrot, peeled
    and thickly sliced
1 medium celery stick,
    chopped
1.5 litres water
freshly ground black
    . pepper
1 × 15 ml spoon
    Worcestershire sauce
salt

Imperial
1 lb ham knuckle, soaked
    overnight
6 oz red lentils
1 large onion, peeled
    and chopped
1 medium carrot, peeled
    and thickly sliced
1 medium celery stick,
    chopped
2½ pints water
freshly ground black
    pepper
1 tablespoon
    Worcestershire sauce
salt

Preparation time: 10 minutes (excluding soaking time)
Cooking time: about 2 hours

Place all the ingredients, except the salt, in a large saucepan and bring slowly to the boil. Skim the surface of the soup with a draining spoon to remove the froth. Reduce the heat, cover the pan and simmer until the ham is cooked.
Remove the knuckle and flake the ham from the bone. Leave the soup to cool slightly. Place the vegetables and liquid in the blender goblet and blend until smooth. Return to the pan, add the ham and reheat for 5 minutes. Adjust the seasoning, adding salt to taste. Serve with croûtons or hot toasted bread.
Serves 6–8

Variations:
Replace the ham knuckle and water with 1.5 litres/ 2½ pints ham stock. Add 50–100 g/2–4 oz cooked ham or bacon, chopped, if available.
Use 4–6 bacon rinds, cut from rashers, instead of the ham knuckle to flavour the soup. Discard before blending.

Fresh tomato soup

Metric
25 g butter
1 large onion, peeled and
    chopped
1 medium carrot, peeled
    and chopped
1 small celery stick
450 g ripe tomatoes
900 ml chicken stock
2 × 15 ml spoons tomato
    purée
salt
freshly ground black
    pepper
1 × 5 ml spoon sugar
1 × 1.25 ml spoon dried
    marjoram

Imperial
1 oz butter
1 large onion, peeled and
    chopped
1 medium carrot, peeled
    and chopped
1 small celery stick
1 lb ripe tomatoes
1½ pints chicken stock
2 tablespoons tomato
    purée
salt
freshly ground black
    pepper
1 teaspoon sugar
¼ teaspoon dried
    marjoram

Preparation time: 10 minutes
Cooking time: about 35 minutes

Melt the butter in a large saucepan, add the onion, carrot and celery and fry gently until soft. Add all the remaining ingredients, with salt and pepper to taste, and bring to the boil. Cover the pan and simmer until the carrot is soft. Leave to cool slightly.
Place the vegetables and liquid in the blender goblet and blend until puréed. Pass the soup through a fine mesh strainer to remove the tomato skin and seeds. Reheat and adjust the seasoning.
Serves 6

Variations:
Add 3 × 15 ml spoons/3 tablespoons cooked rice or pasta to the soup just before serving. Chop the pasta into small pieces if necessary.
Add 1 × 15 ml spoon/1 tablespoon single or double cream, soured cream or plain unsweetened yogurt to the centre of each bowl of soup to garnish.
Use 1 × 400 g/14 oz can peeled tomatoes, undrained, instead of the 450 g/1 lb fresh tomatoes.

Bortsch

Metric
25 g butter
1 large onion, peeled
    and chopped
450 g raw beetroot,
    peeled and chopped
1 medium potato, peeled
    and chopped
900 ml chicken stock
1 × 2.5 ml spoon sugar
4 × 5 ml spoons wine
    vinegar
salt
freshly ground black
    pepper

To serve:
6 × 15 ml spoons soured
    cream
2 × 15 ml spoons chopped
    fresh parsley

Imperial
1 oz butter
1 large onion, peeled
    and chopped
1 lb raw beetroot,
    peeled and chopped
1 medium potato, peeled
    and chopped
1½ pints chicken stock
½ teaspoon sugar
4 teaspoons wine
    vinegar
salt
freshly ground black
    pepper

To serve:
6 tablespoons soured
    cream
2 tablespoons chopped
    fresh parsley

Preparation time: 10 minutes
Cooking time: about 40 minutes

Melt the butter in a large saucepan, add the onion and fry gently until soft. Add all the remaining ingredients, with salt and pepper, and bring to the boil. Cover the pan and simmer until the beetroot is soft. Leave to cool slightly.
Place the vegetables and liquid in the blender goblet and blend until smooth. Adjust the seasoning and add more vinegar, if necessary.
Serve the soup hot or cold with 1 × 15 ml spoon/1 tablespoon soured cream in the centre of each soup bowl and sprinkled with a little chopped parsley.
Serves 6

Variation:
Instead of using chopped raw potato, add 2 × 15 ml spoons/2 tablespoons instant potato at the end of the cooking time.

Smoked haddock soup

Metric
175 g smoked haddock,
    fresh or frozen
25 g butter
1 medium onion, peeled
    and chopped
1 medium potato, peeled
    and roughly chopped
2 medium carrots, peeled
    and chopped
1 large celery stick, cut
    into 3
900 ml water
1 vegetable stock cube
1 small bay leaf
2 × 2.5 cm pieces of
    lemon rind
salt
freshly ground black
    pepper
150 ml double cream

Imperial
6 oz smoked haddock,
    fresh or frozen
1 oz butter
1 medium onion, peeled
    and chopped
1 medium potato, peeled
    and roughly chopped
2 medium carrots, peeled
    and chopped
1 large celery stick, cut
    into 3
1½ pints water
1 vegetable stock cube
1 small bay leaf
2 × 1 inch pieces of
    lemon rind
salt
freshly ground black
    pepper
¼ pint double cream

Preparation time: 10 minutes
Cooking time: about 35 minutes

Simmer the smoked haddock in just enough water to cover for about 10 minutes, or following the packet instructions if using frozen haddock. Leave to cool. Reserve the fish liquor. Remove the skin and flake the fish.
Melt the butter in a large saucepan, add the onion and fry gently until soft. Add all the remaining ingredients, except the salt, pepper, cream and haddock, and bring to the boil. Cover the pan and simmer until the vegetables are soft. Leave to cool slightly.
Remove one-third of the carrot pieces and all the celery. Chop finely, by hand, and reserve. Discard the pieces of lemon rind and the bay leaf. Place the remaining vegetables and the liquid in the blender goblet and blend until smooth. Return to the pan with the flaked fish, reserved fish liquor, chopped vegetables and salt and pepper to taste and reheat. Add the cream just before serving.
Serves 4–6

Variations:
Add a few cooked peeled shrimps or prawns.

From the left: Smoked haddock soup; Bortsch; Mushroom and walnut soup

Mushroom and walnut soup

Preparation time: 10 minutes
Cooking time: 25 minutes

Metric
25 g walnut pieces
25 g butter
1 medium onion, peeled
  and chopped
100 g button mushrooms,
  roughly chopped
900 ml chicken stock
large pinch of grated
  nutmeg
salt
freshly ground black
  pepper
6 × 15 ml spoons double
  cream
6 × 5 ml spoons chopped
  fresh chives, to
  garnish

Imperial
1 oz walnut pieces
1 oz butter
1 medium onion, peeled
  and chopped
4 oz button mushrooms,
  roughly chopped
1½ pints chicken stock
large pinch of grated
  nutmeg
salt
freshly ground black
  pepper
6 tablespoons double
  cream
6 teaspoons chopped
  fresh chives, to
  garnish

Pour sufficient boiling water on to the walnuts to cover and leave for 1 minute. Drain the walnuts and dry on kitchen paper.
Melt the butter in a medium saucepan, add the onion and fry gently until soft. Add the mushrooms and cook for 1 minute. Stir in the stock, nutmeg, salt and pepper to taste and bring to the boil. Cover the pan and simmer for 15 minutes. Leave to cool slightly.
Chop the walnuts in the blender. Add the cooked vegetables and liquid and blend until the mushrooms are finely chopped. Adjust the seasoning. Chill the soup in the refrigerator.
To serve, stir the cream into the soup and sprinkle with the chives.
Serves 4–6

Special chicken liver pâté

Metric	Imperial
50 g butter	*2 oz butter*
1 large onion, peeled and chopped	*1 large onion, peeled and chopped*
1 garlic clove, peeled and crushed	*1 garlic clove, peeled and crushed*
3 streaky bacon rashers, rind removed, chopped	*3 streaky bacon rashers, rind removed, chopped*
100 g mushrooms, roughly chopped	*4 oz mushrooms, roughly chopped*
450 g chicken livers	*1 lb chicken livers*
large pinch of ground allspice or grated nutmeg	*large pinch of ground allspice or grated nutmeg*
salt	*salt*
freshly ground black pepper	*freshly ground black pepper*
1 × 15 ml spoon brandy	*1 tablespoon brandy*

Special chicken liver pâté;
Aubergine appetizer;
Shrimp and crab pâté

Preparation time: about 15 minutes (excluding chilling time)
Cooking time: 12–15 minutes

Melt 25 g/1 oz of the butter in a medium saucepan, add the onion and garlic and fry gently until soft. Add the bacon and cook for 3 minutes, stirring. Add the mushrooms, chicken livers, allspice or nutmeg and salt and pepper to taste and continue cooking, stirring frequently, until the chicken livers are just cooked. Cool slightly.

Place the cooked ingredients and the brandy in the blender goblet and blend until the mixture is smooth. Switch off the motor and scrape down frequently. Add extra melted butter only if the mixture is too stiff after scraping down several times. Adjust the seasoning if necessary.

Turn into a deep 900 ml/1½ pint serving dish. Leave to cool. Melt the remaining butter and cool, then carefully pour it over the top of the pâté. Place in the refrigerator and chill for at least 6 hours before serving. Serve with thin slices of hot toast or crisp crackers.
Serves 6–8

Shrimp and crab pâté

Metric	Imperial
1 × 200 g can peeled shrimps, drained	*1 × 7 oz can peeled shrimps, drained*
2 × 40 g cans dressed crab	*2 × 1½ oz cans dressed crab*
2–3 × 15 ml spoons lemon juice	*2–3 tablespoons lemon juice*
50 g butter, melted	*2 oz butter, melted*
freshly ground black pepper	*freshly ground black pepper*
pinch of cayenne pepper	*pinch of cayenne pepper*
salt (optional)	*salt (optional)*

Preparation time: about 15 minutes (excluding chilling time)

Place all the ingredients, except the salt, in the blender goblet. Blend until a slightly rough consistency is reached. Switch off the motor and scrape down frequently. If preferred, continue blending until the mixture is completely smooth. Adjust the seasoning, adding salt if required. If the pâté is too stiff add extra melted butter or a little single cream. Place the pâté in a 600 ml/1 pint serving bowl and chill for 2 hours.
Serve with hot toast or crisp crackers.
Serves 6

Aubergine appetizer

Metric	Imperial
450 g aubergines, thinly peeled and cut into 2.5 cm cubes	*1 lb aubergines, thinly peeled and cut into 1 inch cubes*
salt	*salt*
3 × 15 ml spoons cooking oil	*3 tablespoons cooking oil*
1 garlic clove, peeled and crushed	*1 garlic clove, peeled and crushed*
1 × 15 ml spoon lemon juice	*1 tablespoon lemon juice*
1 × 1.25 ml spoon chilli sauce	*¼ teaspoon chilli sauce*
freshly ground black pepper	*freshly ground black pepper*
2 × 5 ml spoons powdered gelatine	*2 teaspoons powdered gelatine*
1 × 15 ml spoon cold water	*1 tablespoon cold water*

Preparation time: about 20 minutes (excluding soaking time)
Cooking time: about 20 minutes

Chilli sauce is very hot, so use it cautiously.

Place the aubergine cubes in a colander, sprinkle liberally with salt and leave for about 1 hour, to allow the moisture to come to the surface. Rinse in cold water, drain well and dry with kitchen paper.
Heat the oil in a large frying pan, add the aubergines and garlic and cook gently, stirring occasionally, for about 20 minutes, until soft. Cool slightly. Place the aubergines in the blender goblet and add the lemon juice, chilli sauce and pepper to taste. Blend until smooth. Switch off the motor and scrape down from time to time, if necessary. Taste and adjust the seasoning, adding more salt, pepper, chilli sauce and lemon juice if necessary.
Place the gelatine in a small heatproof basin with the water and leave for about 3 minutes. Stand the basin in a pan of simmering water and leave to dissolve, stirring occasionally. Pour the dissolved gelatine into the aubergine mixture in the blender goblet and blend for a few seconds to combine. Turn the mixture into a deep 600 ml/1 pint serving dish, cover and leave to set in the refrigerator.
Serve with thin slices of hot toast, crisp crackers or small sticks of vegetables such as carrots and celery.
Serves 4–6

MAIN MEALS

A mixer or blender can speed up the preparation time for many main meal dishes. For instance, the mixer makes light work of shortcrust pastry for savoury pies, flans and pasties. It copes with the messy rubbing-in of fat into flour and is much cooler than your hands. Use it, also, to beat boiled potatoes into a smooth cream to pile on top of savoury meat, fish and vegetable mixtures. Sprinkle them with cheese, chopped in the blender, to give a really tasty topping.

The mixer helps with soufflé-making, too. Use it to beat the egg whites, but be careful not to over mix them or they will be difficult to fold into the creamy sauce mixture.

Ham and asparagus mousse

Metric	Imperial
1 × 225 g can asparagus spears	1 × 8 oz can asparagus spears
about 150 ml milk	about ¼ pint milk
25 g butter	1 oz butter
25 g plain flour	1 oz plain flour
2 eggs, separated	2 eggs, separated
100 g full fat soft cheese	4 oz full fat soft cheese
1 × 1.25 ml spoon salt	¼ teaspoon salt
freshly ground white pepper	freshly ground white pepper
15 g gelatine	½ oz gelatine
2 × 15 ml spoons water	2 tablespoons water
175 g lean cooked ham, finely chopped	6 oz lean cooked ham, finely chopped

Preparation time: about 30 minutes (excluding setting time)
Cooking time: about 5 minutes

Drain the asparagus and reserve the juice. Cut 6 of the asparagus spears to about 6 cm/2½ inches in length from the tip, and reserve. Place the remaining asparagus in the blender goblet and blend until puréed. Turn out and reserve.

Make the reserved juice up to 300 ml/½ pint with the milk and pour into the blender goblet. Add the butter and flour. Blend for about 5 seconds until the flour is mixed into the liquid.

Pour into a medium pan and bring slowly to the boil, stirring, until thickened. Cook for 1 minute. Cool slightly. Beat in the egg yolks one at a time. Leave to cool covered closely with cling film or damp greaseproof paper.

Place the soft cheese in the mixer bowl or a large mixing bowl. Using the mixer, beat the soft cheese until smooth, add the sauce mixture, salt and pepper, and beat until well mixed.

Mix the gelatine and water in a small heatproof basin and place in a pan of simmering water until dissolved. Cool slightly and fold into the sauce mixture. Fold in the chopped ham and reserved asparagus purée.

Place the egg whites in the mixer bowl, or a medium mixing bowl. Using the mixer, whisk the whites until just stiff being careful not to over mix or the whites will be difficult to fold in. The tops of the peaks should just fall over when the beaters are lifted from the mixture. Using a metal spoon, fold the whites into the ham mixture. Turn into a deep 1 litre/2 pint serving dish and leave to set. Garnish the top with the reserved asparagus tips.

Ham and asparagus mousse; Plaice with cucumber sauce

Plaice with cucumber sauce

Metric	Imperial
25 g butter, softened	1 oz butter, softened
1 × 1.25 ml spoon grated lemon rind	¼ teaspoon grated lemon rind
1 × 5 ml spoon chopped fresh chives	1 teaspoon chopped fresh chives
salt	salt
freshly ground black pepper	freshly ground black pepper
8 plaice fillets, skinned	8 plaice fillets, skinned
lemon slices, to garnish	lemon slices, to garnish

Cucumber sauce:	**Cucumber sauce:**
15 g butter	½ oz butter
1 small onion, peeled and finely chopped	1 small onion, peeled and finely chopped
1 × 15 cm piece cucumber	1 × 6 inch piece cucumber
150 ml milk	¼ pint milk
8 large parsley sprigs	8 large parsley sprigs
25 g plain flour	1 oz plain flour
2 × 5 ml spoons lemon juice	2 teaspoons lemon juice
salt	salt
freshly ground black pepper	freshly ground black pepper
4 × 15 ml spoons soured cream	4 tablespoons soured cream

Preparation time: 20 minutes
Cooking time: 20 minutes
Oven: 180°C, 350°F, Gas Mark 4

Beat together the butter and lemon rind until creamy. Mix in the chives, and salt and pepper to taste. Rinse the plaice fillets and dry with kitchen paper. Spread chive butter thinly on the skinned side of the fillets. Roll up the fillets and place them in a shallow ovenproof dish. Dot the tops of the fish rolls with any remaining chive butter. Cover with foil and bake in a preheated oven for 20 minutes or until cooked.

Meanwhile, to make the sauce, melt the butter in a saucepan, add the onion and fry gently until soft. Meanwhile cut the cucumber into 2.5 cm/1 inch thick slices, then cut each slice into four. Place the cucumber, milk, parsley sprigs and flour in the blender goblet. Blend until the cucumber and parsley are chopped. Pour the mixture into the pan with the onion and bring to the boil, stirring. Simmer until thickened. Add the lemon juice, and salt and pepper to taste.

Pour off the butter and juices from the plaice into the sauce and mix in. Adjust the seasoning. Stir in the soured cream.

To serve, spoon the sauce over the plaice rolls and garnish with lemon slices.

Mint stuffed chicken with lemon sauce

Metric
1 × 1.5 kg chicken
600 ml water
1 small onion, peeled
   and quartered
Lemon Sauce (page 39),
   to serve

Imperial
1 × 3½ lb chicken
1 pint water
1 small onion, peeled
   and quartered
Lemon Sauce (page 39),
   to serve

For the stuffing:
100 g fresh white
   breadcrumbs
12 large parsley sprigs
24 mint leaves
4 large spring onions,
   finely chopped
1 egg
4 strips lemon rind,
   about 2.5 cm long
1 × 15 ml spoon lemon
   juice
50 g butter, melted
salt
freshly ground black
   pepper

For the stuffing:
4 oz fresh white
   breadcrumbs
12 large parsley sprigs
24 mint leaves
4 large spring onions,
   finely chopped
1 egg
4 strips lemon rind,
   about 1 inch long
1 tablespoon lemon
   juice
2 oz butter, melted
salt
freshly ground black
   pepper

To cook the chicken:
25 g butter, melted
150 ml water

To cook the chicken:
1 oz butter, melted
¼ pint water

Preparation time: 20 minutes
Cooking time: about 1½ hours
Oven: 200°C, 400°F, Gas Mark 6

Remove the giblets from the chicken and place them in a small saucepan with the water and onion. Bring to the boil and simmer for about 30 minutes. Strain and reserve the stock.

For the stuffing, make the breadcrumbs in the blender, adding the parsley and mint at the same time to chop them. Turn into a medium bowl. Add the spring onions to the breadcrumbs. Place the egg and lemon rind and juice in the blender goblet. Blend until the lemon rind is finely chopped. Pour on to the breadcrumb mixture and add the butter and salt and pepper to taste. Combine thoroughly. Use to stuff the neck cavity of the chicken.

Place the chicken in a roasting tin. Pour the melted butter over the chicken, sprinkle with salt and pepper and pour the water into the tin. Roast in a preheated oven for about 1¼ hours or until the chicken is tender. Add additional water if necessary. Use the reserved giblet stock and the stock from the roasting tin to make the lemon sauce.

To serve, carve the chicken and serve with the stuffing and sauce.

Serves 4–6

Variations:
Use the stuffing for a boned shoulder of lamb. Use 1 small onion, peeled and chopped instead of spring onions. Cook in the 50 g/2 oz of butter until softened before adding to the other stuffing ingredients.

Surprise pork chops

Metric	Imperial
4 rib pork chops, cut about 2 cm thick, rind removed	4 rib pork chops, cut about ¾ inch thick, rind removed

For the stuffing:

50 g fresh white breadcrumbs	2 oz fresh white breadcrumbs
10–12 fresh sage leaves	10–12 fresh sage leaves
1 small onion, peeled and cut into pieces	1 small onion, peeled and cut into pieces
1 dessert apple, peeled, cored and cut into pieces	1 dessert apple, peeled, cored and cut into pieces
15 g butter	½ oz butter
4 × 15 ml spoons raisins	4 tablespoons raisins
salt	salt
freshly ground black pepper	freshly ground black pepper

Preparation time: 15 minutes
Cooking time: about 40–50 minutes
Oven: 190°C, 375°F, Gas Mark 5

With a pointed sharp knife, split the pork chops open through the fat towards the rib bone to make a large 'pocket' in them.

Make the breadcrumbs in the blender, adding the sage leaves at the same time to chop them. Turn into a mixing bowl. Feed the onion and apple through the blender lid on to the revolving blades to chop them finely.

Melt the butter in a small frying pan, add the onion and apple mixture and fry gently until soft. Add to the breadcrumbs with the raisins and salt and pepper to taste. Combine thoroughly.

Divide the stuffing into four and use to fill the 'pockets' in the pork chops. Place the chops in a greased baking pan or shallow ovenproof dish. Cook in a preheated oven for 40–50 minutes. Serve with gravy or Spiced Apple Sauce (page 34).

Variation:
Use the stuffing for a boned pork shoulder or leg joint.

Mint stuffed chicken with lemon sauce;
Surprise pork chops; Country beef and potato pie

Country beef and potato pie

Metric	Imperial
1 × 15 ml spoon cooking oil	1 tablespoon cooking oil
1 large onion, peeled and finely chopped	1 large onion, peeled and finely chopped
1 large celery stick, finely chopped	1 large celery stick, finely chopped
750 g minced beef	1½ lb minced beef
1 × 15 ml spoon plain flour	1 tablespoon plain flour
2 × 15 ml spoons tomato purée	2 tablespoons tomato purée
150 ml brown ale or beer	¼ pint brown ale or beer
1 bay leaf	1 bay leaf
salt	salt
freshly ground black pepper	freshly ground black pepper

For the topping:

450 g potatoes, peeled	1 lb potatoes, peeled
225 g parsnips, peeled	8 oz parsnips, peeled
3 × 15 ml spoons milk	3 tablespoons milk
40 g butter	1½ oz butter
salt	salt
freshly ground black pepper	freshly ground black pepper

Preparation time: about 30 minutes
Cooking time: about 1¼ hours
Oven: 180°C, 350°F, Gas Mark 4

Heat the oil in a medium frying pan, add the onion and celery and fry gently until soft. Add the minced beef and cook, stirring, until brown. Stir in the flour and cook for 1 minute. Add the tomato purée, ale or beer, bay leaf and salt and pepper to taste. Bring to the boil, then reduce the heat, cover the pan and simmer for 30 minutes, stirring occasionally.

Meanwhile, prepare the topping. Cook the potatoes and parsnips in boiling salted water until tender. Drain the vegetables and place in the mixer bowl or a large mixing bowl. Using the mixer beat together until smooth. Add the milk, 25 g/1 oz of the butter and salt and pepper to taste and mix in.

Turn the cooked minced beef mixture into a shallow 1.5 litre/2½ pint ovenproof dish. Cover with the potato and parsnip mixture. Melt the remaining butter and brush over the top. Bake in a preheated oven for about 45 minutes or until golden brown.
Serves 4–6

Variations:
Use beef stock instead of ale or beer.
Use swedes or celeriac, peeled, instead of parsnips.

Shortcrust pastry

Metric	Imperial
150 g plain flour	6 oz plain flour
large pinch of salt	large pinch of salt
75 g butter and lard, or	3 oz butter and lard, or
margarine and lard	margarine and lard
2 × 15 ml spoons cold	2 tablespoons cold
water	water

Preparation time: about 5 minutes

Place the flour and salt in the mixer bowl or a large mixing bowl. Cut the fat into about 1 cm/½ inch cubes and add to the flour. Using a low speed on the mixer, rub the fat into the flour until the mixture resembles fine breadcrumbs. Add the water using the mixer, or by hand, to form a firm dough. Turn out on to a floured surface and knead lightly until smooth. Use to line a 20 cm/8 inch flan ring.

Variations:

For wholemeal or wheatmeal pastry, replace the plain flour with wholemeal or wheatmeal flour.

For cheese pastry, add 1 × 2.5 ml spoon/½ teaspoon dry mustard to the flour, rub in the fat and add 75 g/ 3 oz finely chopped, or grated Cheddar cheese. To chop the cheese in the blender, cut the cheese into small pieces and drop through the centre of the lid on to revolving blades.

Smoked haddock and parsley quiche

Metric	Imperial
250 g Shortcrust Pastry (above)	9 oz Shortcrust Pastry (above)
225 g smoked haddock, cooked, skinned and flaked	8 oz smoked haddock, cooked, skinned and flaked
2 eggs	2 eggs
150 ml single cream	¼ pint single cream
4 × 15 ml spoons milk	4 tablespoons milk
6 sprigs parsley	6 sprigs parsley
1 × 1.25 ml spoon salt	¼ teaspoon salt
freshly ground black pepper	freshly ground black pepper

Preparation time: 15 minutes
Cooking time: about 25 minutes
Oven temperatute: 200°C, 400°F, Gas Mark 6

Roll out the pastry into a 25 cm/10 inch circle and line a 20 cm/8 inch flan ring on a baking tray or a flan dish.

Place the flaked haddock in the pastry case. Place all the remaining ingredients in the blender goblet and blend for 5–10 seconds until the parsley is chopped. Pour into the pastry case.

Bake in a preheated oven for about 25 minutes until the pastry is cooked and the filling just set.
Serves 4–6

Variation:

Replace half of the smoked haddock with 100 g/4 oz peeled prawns or shrimps.

Salami and pepper quiche

Metric	Imperial
250 g Shortcrust Pastry (above)	9 oz Shortcrust Pastry (above)
50 g salami or ham, finely chopped	2 oz salami or ham, finely chopped
2 eggs	2 eggs
100 g full fat soft cheese	4 oz full fat soft cheese
150 ml milk	¼ pint milk
1 small red pepper, cored, seeded and roughly chopped	1 small red pepper, cored, seeded and roughly chopped
3 spring onions	3 spring onions
1 × 1.25 ml spoon salt	¼ teaspoon salt
freshly ground black pepper	freshly ground black pepper

Preparation time: 15 minutes
Cooking time: about 25 minutes
Oven temperature: 200°C, 400°F, Gas Mark 6

Roll out the pastry into a 25 cm/10 inch circle and line a 20 cm/8 inch flan ring on a baking sheet or a flan dish.

Place the chopped salami or ham in the pastry case. Place all the remaining ingredients in the blender goblet and blend for 5–10 seconds until the pepper is finely chopped. Pour into the pastry case.

Bake in a preheated oven for about 25 minutes until the pastry is cooked and the filling set.
Serves 4–6

Mushroom and onion quiche

Metric
250 g Shortcrust Pastry (opposite)
15 g butter
1 large onion, peeled and thinly sliced
50 g Cheddar cheese, cut into small pieces
150 ml milk or single cream
2 eggs
1 × 1.25 spoon salt
freshly ground black pepper
100 g button mushrooms

Imperial
9 oz Shortcrust Pastry (opposite)
½ oz butter
1 large onion, peeled and thinly sliced
2 oz Cheddar cheese, cut into small pieces
¼ pint milk or single cream
2 eggs
¼ teaspoon salt
freshly ground black pepper
4 oz button mushrooms

Preparation time: 15 minutes
Cooking time: about 25 minutes
Oven temperature: 200°C, 400°F, Gas Mark 6

Roll out the pastry into a 25 cm/10 inch circle and line a 20 cm/8 inch flan ring on a baking sheet or a flan dish.
Melt the butter in a medium pan, add the onion and cook gently for about 5 minutes, until soft but not brown. Cool slightly and place in the pastry case.
Drop the cheese through the centre of the blender lid on to revolving blades. Turn out and reserve.
Place the milk, eggs, salt and pepper in the blender goblet. Reserve 3 mushrooms and add the remaining mushrooms to the blender. Blend for 5–10 seconds until the mushrooms are finely chopped. Pour into the pastry case. Thinly slice the reserved mushrooms and scatter on top. Sprinkle with the cheese.
Bake in a preheated oven for about 25 minutes until the pastry is cooked and the filling just set.
Serves 4–6

Variation:
Replace the onion with 50 g/2 oz chopped cooked ham or bacon.

From the front, clockwise: Salami and pepper quiche;
Smoked haddock and parsley quiche;
Mushroom and onion quiche

Chicken, tongue and tomato moulds

Metric	Imperial
450 g ripe tomatoes, cut into quarters	1 lb ripe tomatoes, cut into quarters
½ small green pepper, cored, seeds removed, roughly chopped	½ small green pepper, cored, seeds removed, roughly chopped
½ small onion, peeled and chopped	½ small onion, peeled and chopped
10 cm length cucumber, chopped	4 inch length cucumber, chopped
1 small celery stick, cut into 4 or 5 pieces	1 small celery stick, cut into 4 or 5 pieces
1 × 2.5 ml spoon salt	½ teaspoon salt
1 × 1.25 ml spoon pepper	¼ teaspoon pepper
1 × 1.25 ml spoon sugar	¼ teaspoon sugar
1 × 5 ml spoon wine vinegar	1 teaspoon wine vinegar
2 large pinches dried basil	2 large pinches dried basil
15 g gelatine	½ oz gelatine
150 ml chicken stock	¼ pint chicken stock
225 g cooked chicken, coarsely chopped	8 oz cooked chicken, coarsely chopped
100 g pressed tongue, coarsely chopped	4 oz pressed tongue, coarsely chopped

Preparation time: about 25 minutes (excluding setting time)

Place the tomatoes, pepper, onion, cucumber and celery in the blender goblet and blend until puréed. It will be necessary to purée in two or three batches. Pass the purée through a fine nylon strainer to remove the tomato seeds and skin. Add the salt, pepper, sugar, vinegar and basil.
Mix the gelatine with 2 × 15 ml spoons/2 tablespoons of the chicken stock in a small basin and place in a pan of simmering water until dissolved. Cool slightly. Add the remaining chicken stock to the tomato mixture and stir in the gelatine. Leave until just beginning to set. Mix in the chicken and tongue. Pour into a 1.2 litre/2 pint mould, or six 150 ml/¼ pint individual moulds and leave to set.
To turn out, dip the mould into warm water for a few seconds and invert on to a serving plate.
Serve with a mixed green salad.
Serves 6

Variation:
Replace the chicken with turkey and/or replace the tongue with cooked ham.

Crusty cheese and onion soufflé

Metric	Imperial
8 slices French bread, cut 1 cm thick	8 slices French bread, cut ½ inch thick
50 g butter, softened	2 oz butter, softened

For the soufflé:	**For the soufflé:**
100 g mature Cheddar cheese	4 oz mature Cheddar cheese
25 g butter	1 oz butter
1 medium onion, peeled and finely chopped	1 medium onion, peeled and finely chopped
150 ml milk	¼ pint milk
25 g plain flour	1 oz plain flour
1 × 5 ml spoon made mustard	1 teaspoon made mustard
salt	salt
freshly ground black pepper	freshly ground black pepper
3 eggs, separated	3 eggs, separated

Preparation time: about 25 minutes
Cooking time: about 30 minutes
Oven: 200°C, 400°F, Gas Mark 6

Spread both sides of the bread slices with the softened butter. Lightly butter the bottom and sides of a 900 ml/1½ pint soufflé dish. Line the sides of the dish with the bread slices. Stand the dish on a baking sheet. For the soufflé, cut the cheese into small pieces and drop through the centre of the blender lid on to revolving blades to chop it. Melt the butter in a medium saucepan, add the onion and fry gently until soft.
Pour the milk into the blender goblet and add the flour, mustard and salt and pepper to taste. Blend for about 5 seconds to mix in the flour. Pour into the pan with the onion and bring to the boil, stirring constantly. Simmer until thickened. Remove from the heat and mix in the cheese until it has melted. Cool slightly, then beat in the egg yolks.
Place the egg whites in the mixer bowl or large mixing bowl and whisk until just stiff. Carefully fold about 2 large spoonfuls of the sauce mixture into the egg whites. Add the remaining sauce and fold in. Turn the soufflé mixture into the prepared dish, being careful not to dislodge the bread slices. Bake immediately in a preheated oven for about 30 minutes or until well risen and golden brown. Serve at once.

Chicken, tongue and tomato moulds;
Crusty cheese and onion soufflé

PUDDINGS

The preparation of hot and cold soufflés, mousses and meringue toppings for flans and fruit is speeded up with a mixer to cope with all the whisking jobs.

Fruit purées made in the blender can be used in many puddings. Add them to soufflés, mousses and plain unsweetened yogurt to give a real fruit flavour or serve them hot as a different and mouthwatering sauce for steamed puddings and pancakes.

Home-made ice cream is so delicious, and flavoured with a blender-prepared fresh fruit purée it becomes very special. Fresh fruit purées, such as raspberry, strawberry and blackberry make excellent fruit sorbets, too.

Zabaglione

Metric	Imperial
4 egg yolks	4 egg yolks
2 egg whites	2 egg whites
4 × 15 ml spoons caster sugar	4 tablespoons caster sugar
4 × 15 ml spoons Marsala or sweet sherry	4 tablespoons Marsala or sweet sherry

Preparation time: 3 minutes
Cooking time: about 5 minutes

Use a large heatproof pottery or glass mixing bowl, about 2.5 litre/4½ pint capacity, and a large saucepan into which the bowl will sit. Add sufficient water to the pan so that the base of the bowl will be immersed in water. Remove the bowl from the pan. Bring the water to the boil, then reduce to simmering point.
Put all the ingredients in the bowl and place over the pan of simmering water. Using a hand mixer, whisk on the highest speed until the mixture is very thick, frothy and leaves a trail when the beaters are held out of the mixture. (Switch off the mixer before lifting out of the mixture.) This will take about 5 minutes. Do not allow the water in the pan to boil or the mixture will cook on the sides of the bowl and a poor volume will result.
Serve immediately in large individual glasses. Hand thin biscuits, wafers or shortbread fingers separately.
Serves 4–6

Lemon and strawberry cheesecake

Metric
225 g cottage cheese
4 × 15 ml spoons lemon
  juice
150 ml double cream
2 eggs, separated
2 × 5 ml spoons grated
  lemon rind
100 g caster sugar
15 g powdered gelatine
2 × 15 ml spoons water

For the biscuit crust:
75 g digestive biscuits
40 g butter, melted
1 × 15 ml spoon demerara
  sugar
225 g strawberries, to
  decorate

Imperial
8 oz cottage cheese
4 tablespoons lemon
  juice
¼ pint double cream
2 eggs, separated
2 teaspoons grated
  lemon rind
4 oz caster sugar
½ oz powdered gelatine
2 tablespoons water

For the biscuit crust:
3 oz digestive biscuits
1½ oz butter, melted
1 tablespoon demerara
  sugar
8 oz strawberries, to
  decorate

Preparation time: about 30 minutes (excluding setting time)

Place the cottage cheese and lemon juice in the blender goblet and blend until smooth. Stop the motor and scrape down the mixture, if necessary.

Place the cream in the mixer bowl, or a medium mixing bowl. Using the mixer, whisk until the cream is just stiff, being careful not to over mix. If using a table mixer transfer the cream to another bowl.

Place the egg yolks, lemon rind and sugar in the mixer bowl, or a large mixing bowl. Using the mixer, whisk until the mixture is light and creamy. Whisk in the blended cottage cheese.

Mix the gelatine and water in a small heatproof basin and place in a pan of simmering water until dissolved. Cool slightly and whisk into the cottage cheese mixture. If using a table mixer transfer the mixture to a large mixing bowl.

Ensure that the mixer bowl and beaters are free from all traces of grease. Place the egg whites in the mixer bowl or a medium mixing bowl. Using the mixer, whisk the whites until just stiff being careful not to over mix. The tops of the peaks should just fall over when the beaters are lifted from the mixture.

Reserve half the whipped cream for decoration. Fold the remaining cream into the cheese mixture. Using a metal spoon, fold in the egg whites. Turn into a 20 cm/8 inch sandwich tin and leave to set.

To make the biscuit crust, break the biscuits into pieces and drop through the centre of the blender lid on to revolving blades to make crumbs. Stir into the melted butter with the sugar. Spread evenly over the surface of the set cheesecake, pressing down gently. Leave to become firm.

To turn out, loosen the edge of the cheesecake with a palette knife. Dip the base of the tin into warm water for a few seconds, place the serving plate over the top of the tin and invert the tin and plate.

Use the reserved whipped cream and the strawberries to decorate the top.

Serves 6–8

Variations:
Replace half the lemon juice and rind with orange juice and rind.

Use raspberries, blackberries, grapes, halved and pips removed, sliced fresh peaches dipped in lemon juice, instead of strawberries.

Zabaglione; Lemon and strawberry cheesecake

Hot apricot soufflé with Seville sauce

Metric	Imperial
1 × 425 g can apricot halves	1 × 15 oz can apricot halves
150 ml milk	¼ pint milk
25 g plain flour	1 oz plain flour
25 g butter	1 oz butter
50 g caster sugar	2 oz caster sugar
almond essence	almond essence
3 eggs (sizes 1, 2), or 4 smaller eggs, separated	3 eggs (sizes 1, 2), or 4 smaller eggs, separated

For the sauce:	For the sauce:
2 × 5 ml spoons cornflour	2 teaspoons cornflour
2 × 15 ml spoons marmalade	2 tablespoons marmalade
2 × 15 ml spoons sugar	2 tablespoons sugar
4 × 15 ml spoons sweet sherry	4 tablespoons sweet sherry

Preparation time: about 20 minutes
Cooking time: about 45 minutes
Oven: 190°C, 375°F, Gas Mark 5

Drain the juice from the apricots and reserve. Place the apricots and 2 × 15 ml spoons/2 tablespoons of the reserved juice in the blender goblet. Blend until puréed. Turn out into a small bowl.

Place the milk, flour and butter in the blender goblet and blend for a few seconds until mixed. Pour into a medium saucepan and bring to the boil, stirring, until thickened. Cook over a low heat for 1 minute. The sauce should be very thick. Mix in the sugar, a few drops of almond essence and the apricot purée. Cool slightly, then beat in the egg yolks, one at a time.

Place the egg whites in the mixer bowl or a large mixing bowl. Using the mixer, whisk the whites until just stiff. The tops of the peaks should just fall over when the beaters are lifted out of the mixture.

Using a metal spoon, gently fold about 2 large spoonfuls of the sauce mixture into the whites. Add the remaining sauce and fold in. Turn into a well-buttered 1.2 litre/2 pint soufflé dish, or straight-sided ovenproof dish, and place in the centre of a preheated oven. Bake for about 45 minutes or until well risen and golden brown.

Meanwhile, to make the sauce, measure the remaining apricot juice and make it up to 150 ml/¼ pint with water if necessary. Place the apricot juice, cornflour and marmalade in the blender goblet and blend for a few seconds until mixed. Pour into a small saucepan, add the sugar and bring to the boil, stirring, until thickened. Add the sherry. Reheat before serving.

To serve, remove the soufflé from the oven and serve immediately. Hand the sauce separately.

Iced summer puddings

Metric	Imperial
For the ice cream:	For the ice cream:
75 g granulated sugar	3 oz granulated sugar
300 ml double cream	½ pint double cream
3 × 15 ml spoons brandy	3 tablespoons brandy
3 egg whites	3 egg whites
100 g fresh brown breadcrumbs	4 oz fresh brown breadcrumbs

For the raspberry sauce:	For the raspberry sauce:
450 g fresh or frozen and thawed raspberries, or a mixture of strawberries and raspberries	1 lb fresh or frozen and thawed raspberries or a mixture of strawberries and raspberries
2 × 15 ml spoons sugar	2 tablespoons sugar
a little water, orange juice or white wine (optional)	a little water, orange juice or white wine (optional)

Preparation time: 20 minutes (excluding freezing time)

Use the blender to grind the sugar until it looks like icing sugar. Reserve.

Place the cream in the mixer bowl or a large mixing bowl. Using the mixer, whip until the cream is just stiff. Be careful not to over mix. Whisk in the brandy. If using a table mixer, transfer the cream to a large mixing bowl.

Ensure that the mixing bowl and beaters are free from all traces of grease. Place the egg whites in the mixer bowl or large mixing bowl. Using the mixer whisk until very stiff. Gradually whisk in the prepared sugar. Fold the breadcrumbs into the cream by hand, followed by the egg whites.

Turn into 10–12 individual 150 ml/¼ pint freezerproof moulds or 1 × 1.6 litre/2¾ pint freezerproof mould, basin or container. Place in the freezer or freezing compartment of a refrigerator and freeze until completely frozen.

To make the sauce, place the berries in the blender goblet with the sugar. Blend until puréed. Add extra sugar to taste. Pass through a fine nylon strainer to remove the pips. Stir in a little water, orange juice or white wine if the sauce is too thick. Chill.

To serve, unmould the ice cream and serve with the sauce poured over.

Serves 10–12

From the front: Hot apricot soufflé with Seville sauce; Iced summer puddings; Blackcurrant parfait

Blackcurrant parfait

Metric	**Imperial**
225 g blackcurrants, fresh or frozen	8 oz blackcurrants, fresh or frozen
1 × 15 ml spoon water	1 tablespoon water
50 g granulated sugar	2 oz granulated sugar
150 ml double cream	¼ pint double cream
1 × 175 g can evaporated milk, well chilled	1 × 6 oz can evaporated milk, well chilled
2 eggs, separated	2 eggs, separated
50 g caster sugar	2 oz caster sugar

Preparation time: about 30 minutes (excluding freezing time)
Cooking time: 5 minutes

Place the blackcurrants, water and granulated sugar in a medium pan, bring to the boil, reduce the heat, cover and simmer for 5 minutes. Leave to cool. Place in the blender goblet and blend until puréed. Pass through a fine nylon strainer to remove the seeds.

Place the cream in the mixer bowl or a medium mixing bowl. Using the mixer, whisk until the cream is just stiff. If using a table mixer, transfer the cream to a large mixing bowl.

Place the evaporated milk in the mixer bowl or a large mixing bowl. Using the mixer, whisk until the milk thickens. It will take 3–5 minutes. Whisk in the egg yolks, one at a time. Reduce the mixer speed and mix in the blackcurrant purée. Stop the mixer and scrape down the sides of the bowl. Using the lowest speed fold in the cream. Alternatively, fold in the cream by hand. If using a table mixer transfer the blackcurrant mixture to a large mixing bowl.

Place the egg whites in the mixing bowl or a medium mixing bowl. Ensure that the mixing bowl and beaters are free from all traces of grease otherwise the egg whites will not become stiff during whisking. Using the mixer, whisk the whites until just stiff, being careful not to over mix. The tops of the peaks should just fall over when the beaters are lifted out of the bowl. Add the caster sugar and whisk for 20 seconds. Fold the whites into the blackcurrant mixture by hand using a metal spoon.

Place in a 1.5 litre/2½ pint container and put in a freezer or freezing compartment of a refrigerator until completely frozen. There is no need to beat this ice cream during freezing.
Serves 6–8

Variation:
Replace fresh or frozen blackcurrants with a 300 g/10 oz can of blackcurrants, but omit the granulated sugar and initial simmering. Place the blackcurrants and the juice in the blender and purée as above.

Melon and lime sorbet

Metric	Imperial
175 g sugar	6 oz sugar
5 × 15 ml spoons water	5 tablespoons water
450 g ripe melon, weighed without skin and seeds, chopped	1 lb ripe melon, weighed without skin and seeds, chopped
3 × 15 ml spoons fresh lime juice	3 tablespoons fresh lime juice
2 egg whites	2 egg whites

Preparation time: 20 minutes (excluding freezing time)
Cooking time: 10 minutes

Place the sugar and water in a saucepan and heat gently to dissolve the sugar, stirring. Make sure the sugar has dissolved before the syrup boils. Allow to boil gently for 10 minutes. Cool slightly.

Meanwhile, put the melon pieces in the blender goblet and blend until puréed. If the melon is ripe it should not be necessary to add any liquid. Prepare in batches, if necessary. Add the lime juice to the purée and stir in the sugar syrup. Leave to cool.

Pour the cooled mixture into a 1.5 litre/2½ pint shallow polythene container and freeze until half frozen and mushy in consistency.

Place the egg whites in the mixer bowl or a medium mixing bowl. Using the mixer, whisk until just stiff, being careful not to over mix or the whites will be difficult to fold in. The tops of the peaks should just fall over when the beaters are lifted out of the mixture. Whisk the half-frozen fruit mixture until the ice particles are broken up evenly. Fold in the whites by hand. Turn into the container and freeze until completely frozen.
Serves 6–8

Variation:
Replace fresh lime juice with 150 ml/¼ pint lime cordial; omit the water and reduce the sugar to 150 g/5 oz, dissolved in the lime cordial instead of water.

Pineapple sorbet

Metric	Imperial
175 g granulated sugar	6 oz granulated sugar
300 ml water	½ pint water
1 medium fresh, ripe pineapple (about 450 g flesh)	1 medium fresh, ripe pineapple (about 1 lb flesh)
3 × 15 ml spoons lemon juice	3 tablespoons lemon juice
2 egg whites	2 egg whites

Preparation time: about 15 minutes (excluding freezing time)
Cooking time: 5 minutes

Put the sugar and water in a medium pan and place over a low heat to dissolve the sugar. Increase the heat and boil gently for 5 minutes. Leave to cool.

To prepare the pineapple, remove the outside covering with a sharp knife. Slice the pineapple, remove the centre core and roughly chop the flesh.

Place the pineapple in the blender goblet with sufficient of the cooled syrup to nearly cover the pieces. Blend until puréed. It may be necessary to purée in 2 or 3 batches. Combine the pineapple purée, remaining syrup and lemon juice. Pour into a 1.5 litre/2½ pint shallow, polythene container and place in the freezer until half frozen and mushy in consistency. Scrape down the frozen mixture from the sides once or twice during freezing.

Place the egg whites in the mixer bowl, or a medium mixing bowl. Using the mixer whisk the whites until just stiff. The tops of the peaks should just fall over when the beaters are lifted out of the mixture. Be careful not to over mix or the whites will be difficult to fold in. Whisk the half frozen fruit mixture until the ice particles are broken up evenly. Fold in the egg whites by hand. Return the container to the freezer until the mixture is completely frozen.
Serves 8

Gooseberry mousse

Metric
1 × 425 g can gooseberries
2 × 15 ml spoons sugar
15 g powdered gelatine
3 × 15 ml spoons water
150 ml double cream
2 egg whites

Imperial
1 × 15 oz can gooseberries
2 tablespoons sugar
½ oz powdered gelatine
3 tablespoons water
¼ pint double cream
2 egg whites

To decorate:
whipped cream
chopped nuts

To decorate:
whipped cream
chopped nuts

Melon and lime sorbet; Pineapple sorbet; Gooseberry mousse

Preparation time: 15 minutes (excluding setting time)

Place the gooseberries, with the can juice and sugar, in the blender goblet and blend until puréed. Pass through a fine nylon strainer to remove the pips.
Place the gelatine in a small heatproof basin with the water and leave for about 3 minutes. Stand the basin in a pan of simmering water and leave to dissolve, stirring occasionally. Stir the gelatine into the gooseberry purée. Chill in the refrigerator until the mixture is beginning to set.
Using the mixer, whip the cream until just stiff. Fold the gooseberry mixture into the cream by hand.
Ensure that the mixer bowl and beaters are free from all traces of grease. Place the egg whites in the mixer bowl or large mixing bowl. Whisk the whites until just stiff, being careful not to over mix or the whites will be too stiff to fold in. The tops of the peaks should just fall over when the beaters are lifted out of the mixture.
Fold the whites into the gooseberry and cream mixture by hand. Spoon into a 1.2 litre/2 pint mould or serving bowl. Leave to set in the refrigerator.
Serve decorated with cream and chopped nuts.
Serves 6

Variations:
Use other canned fruits, such as apricots, raspberries or plums, instead of gooseberries.

Mocha hazelnut ice cream ⊠

Metric	Imperial
75 g granulated sugar	3 oz granulated sugar
2 × 5 ml spoons instant coffee powder	2 teaspoons instant coffee powder
1 × 15 ml spoon boiling water	1 tablespoon boiling water
150 ml double cream	¼ pint double cream
3 eggs, separated	3 eggs, separated
150 ml plain unsweetened yogurt	5 fl oz plain unsweetened yogurt
50 g hazelnuts, chopped in the blender	2 oz hazelnuts, chopped in the blender
50 g plain chocolate, chopped	2 oz plain chocolate, chopped

Preparation time: about 15 minutes (excluding freezing time)

Use the blender to grind the sugar until it looks like icing sugar. Reserve. Dissolve the coffee in the boiling water and leave to cool.

Place the cream in the mixer bowl or a large mixing bowl. Using the mixer, whip until the cream is just stiff. Be careful not to over mix. Whisk in the egg yolks, one at a time. Fold in the yogurt, nuts and chocolate on the lowest mixer speed and switch off immediately the ingredients are combined. Alternatively, fold in by hand. If using a table mixer, transfer the mixture to a large bowl.

Ensure that the mixing bowl and beaters are free from all traces of grease. Place the egg whites in the mixer bowl and whisk until very stiff. Gradually whisk in the prepared sugar. Fold the egg whites into the cream mixture by hand.

Turn the mixture into a 1.5 litre/2½ pint freezerproof container and place in the freezer or the freezing compartment of the refrigerator. Freeze until completely frozen. There is no need to beat this ice cream during freezing.

Serve with Dark Chocolate Sauce (page 43) or decorated with piped whipped cream.

Serves 6–8

Variations:

Use walnuts instead of hazelnuts.

For a plain ice cream, omit the chocolate, nuts and coffee mixture and flavour with a few drops of vanilla essence instead.

Coffee and brandy soufflé ⊠

Metric	Imperial
300 ml double cream	½ pint double cream
15 g powdered gelatine	½ oz powdered gelatine
3 × 15 ml spoons water	3 tablespoons water
4 eggs, separated	4 eggs, separated
100 g caster sugar	4 oz caster sugar
2 × 15 ml spoons coffee essence, or 1 × 15 ml spoon instant coffee dissolved in 2 × 15 ml spoons boiling water	2 tablespoons coffee essence, or 1 tablespoon instant coffee dissolved in 2 tablespoons boiling water
2 × 15 ml spoons brandy	2 tablespoons brandy

To decorate:	To decorate:
finely chopped walnuts whipped cream	finely chopped walnuts whipped cream

Preparation time: about 35 minutes (excluding setting time)

Tie a band of double thickness greaseproof paper around the outside of a 900 ml/1½ pint soufflé dish. The paper collar should stand about 5 cm/2 inches above the top of the dish.

Place the double cream in the mixer bowl, or a medium mixing bowl. Using the mixer, whisk until just thick, being careful not to over mix. If using a mixer bowl transfer the cream to another bowl. Place the gelatine in a small heatproof basin with the water and leave for about 3 minutes. Stand in a pan of simmering water until dissolved, stirring occasionally. Put the egg yolks in a large heatproof mixing bowl. Add the sugar, coffee essence or dissolved coffee and brandy and place the bowl over a pan of simmering water. Using a hand mixer, or hand whisk, whisk the yolks until very thick and creamy. Remove from the heat, whisk in the dissolved gelatine and continue whisking until the mixture is cool.

Ensure that the mixer bowl and beaters are free from all traces of grease. Put the egg whites in the mixer bowl or large mixing bowl. Using the mixer, whisk the egg whites until they are just stiff; be careful not to over mix. The tops of the peaks should just fall over when the beaters are drawn out of the mixture.

Using a large metal spoon, fold the whipped cream into the egg yolk mixture, followed by the egg whites. Turn into the prepared soufflé dish, place in the refrigerator and leave to set.

To serve, remove the paper collar carefully, using a knife to help. Coat the sides of the soufflé with the chopped walnuts and decorate the top with cream.

Serves 6–8

Mocha hazelnut ice cream; Coffee and brandy soufflé

SAUCES AND SALAD DRESSINGS

Making a sauce is quick and easy with a blender. Delicious vegetable and fruit-based sauces are simply made by puréeing cooked vegetables or fruit in the blender. Remember that if the vegetable or fruit has small seeds or pips they will not disappear during blending but are easily removed by sieving the purée. A fruity sauce makes all the difference to a plain steamed or baked sponge pudding and turns ice cream into a fabulous dessert. Use fruit in season, or canned. All the high water content fresh fruits (such as strawberries, raspberries or blackberries) can be puréed raw, with just a little sugar added to bring out the flavour.

Salad dressings are made in seconds and a variety of flavourings from fresh herbs to blue cheese can be added to the basic dressing ingredients.

Spiced apple sauce

Metric	*Imperial*
15 g butter	½ oz butter
1 small onion, peeled and chopped	1 small onion, peeled and chopped
450 g cooking apples, peeled, cored and roughly sliced	1 lb cooking apples, peeled, cored and roughly sliced
1 × 15 ml spoon water	1 tablespoon water
1 × 15 ml spoon Worcestershire sauce	1 tablespoon Worcestershire sauce
1 × 15 ml spoon lemon juice	1 tablespoon lemon juice
1 × 15 ml spoon sugar	1 tablespoon sugar

Preparation time: 10 minutes
Cooking time: 15 minutes

Serve warm or cold with roast pork or grilled pork chops, baked or boiled ham or bacon, roast duck, or grilled or fried sausages.

Melt the butter in a medium saucepan, add the onion and fry gently until soft. Add all the remaining ingredients and stir well. Cover the pan and cook over a low heat for 10 minutes or until the apple is soft. Cool slightly. Pour into the blender goblet and blend until smooth.

Store any leftover sauce in a tightly covered container in the refrigerator or freezer for up to 1 week or 6 months, respectively.

Serves 6

Barbecue sauce or baste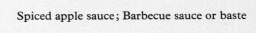

Preparation time: 10 minutes
Cooking time: 25 minutes

Brush over pork spareribs, chicken, kebabs, sausages or beefburgers halfway through the cooking time, or serve separately as a sauce.

Metric
1 × 15 ml spoon cooking oil
1 medium onion, peeled and chopped
1 garlic clove, peeled and crushed
1 × 225 g can tomatoes
1 × 15 ml spoon tomato purée
1 × 5 ml spoon mixed spice
1 × 5 ml spoon ground ginger
1 × 5 ml spoon dry mustard
1 × 15 ml spoon soft brown sugar
1 × 15 ml spoon Worcestershire sauce
2 × 15 ml spoons wine vinegar
salt
freshly ground black pepper

Imperial
1 tablespoon cooking oil
1 medium onion, peeled and chopped
1 garlic clove, peeled and crushed
1 × 8 oz can tomatoes
1 tablespoon tomato purée
1 teaspoon mixed spice
1 teaspoon ground ginger
1 teaspoon dry mustard
1 tablespoon soft brown sugar
1 tablespoon Worcestershire sauce
2 tablespoons wine vinegar
salt
freshly ground black pepper

Heat the oil in a medium saucepan, add the onion and garlic and fry gently until soft. Add the tomatoes with the can juice and all the remaining ingredients with salt and pepper to taste. Bring to the boil, stirring well, then cover the pan and simmer for 15 minutes. Cool slightly.
Pour into the blender goblet and blend until smooth. Adjust the seasoning, adding extra salt, pepper, vinegar and sugar to taste.
To use as a baste add an extra 1 × 15 ml spoon/ 1 tablespoon oil.
To use as a sauce add 2–3 × 15 ml spoons/2–3 table-spoons water or chicken stock to thin down the mixture. Adjust the seasoning again.
Serves 4–6

Spiced apple sauce ; Barbecue sauce or baste

Tomato sauce

Metric
25 g butter
1 medium onion, peeled and chopped
1 garlic clove, peeled and crushed
450 g ripe tomatoes, roughly chopped
3 × 15 ml spoons water or chicken stock
2 × 15 ml spoons tomato purée
2 rinds cut from bacon rashers (optional)
1 × 5 ml spoon brown sugar
1 × 2.5 ml spoon dried basil
salt
freshly ground black pepper
1 × 15 ml spoon wine vinegar

Imperial
1 oz butter
1 medium onion, peeled and chopped
1 garlic clove, peeled and crushed
1 lb ripe tomatoes, roughly chopped
3 tablespoons water or chicken stock
2 tablespoons tomato purée
2 rinds cut from bacon rashers (optional)
1 teaspoon brown sugar
½ teaspoon dried basil
salt
freshly ground black pepper
1 tablespoon wine vinegar

Preparation time: 15 minutes
Cooking time: 35 minutes

Serve with a meat loaf, grilled or fried chicken or sausages, or grilled or fried fish.

Melt the butter in a medium saucepan. Add the onion and garlic and fry gently until soft. Add all the remaining ingredients, except the vinegar. Bring to the boil, stirring well, then cover the pan and simmer for 30 minutes. Cool slightly.
Remove the bacon rinds, if used. Pour the sauce into the blender goblet and blend until smooth. Pass the sauce through a sieve to remove the tomato skins and seeds. Return to the pan, add the vinegar and reheat. Adjust the seasoning, adding extra salt, pepper, sugar and vinegar to taste.
Serves 4–6

Variation:
Use 1 × 425 g/15 oz can peeled tomatoes, undrained, instead of fresh tomatoes. Omit the water or stock.

Peperoni sauce

Metric
1 × 15 ml spoon cooking oil
1 medium onion, peeled and chopped
1 small garlic clove, peeled and crushed
1 medium green pepper, cored, seeded and roughly chopped
1 medium red pepper, cored, seeded and roughly chopped
1 × 225 g can tomatoes
1 × 15 ml spoon tomato purée
salt
freshly ground black pepper

Imperial
1 tablespoon cooking oil
1 medium onion, peeled and chopped
1 small garlic clove, peeled and crushed
1 medium green pepper, cored, seeded and roughly chopped
1 medium red pepper, cored, seeded and roughly chopped
1 × 8 oz can tomatoes
1 tablespoon tomato purée
salt
freshly ground black pepper

Preparation time: 10 minutes
Cooking time: 25 minutes

Serve with fried or grilled chicken, pork or lamb chops or white fish; spoon over omelettes, scrambled eggs or hard-boiled eggs; use as a coating sauce for cauliflower or courgettes.

Heat the oil in a medium saucepan, add the onion and garlic and fry gently until soft. Add the green and red peppers and cook for 2 minutes. Add the tomatoes with the can juice and all the remaining ingredients with salt and pepper to taste. Bring to the boil, stirring well, then cover the pan and simmer for 15 minutes. Cool slightly. Pour into the blender goblet and blend until smooth. Return to the pan and reheat. Adjust the seasoning.
Serves 4–6

Variations:
Add 1 × 1.25 ml spoon/¼ teaspoon, or more, chilli sauce to make a 'hot' sauce.

From the front: Hollandaise sauce;
Peperoni sauce; Tomato sauce

Hollandaise sauce

Metric	Imperial
3 egg yolks	*3 egg yolks*
1 × 15 ml spoon water	*1 tablespoon water*
2 × 15 ml spoons lemon juice	*2 tablespoons lemon juice*
2 × 15 ml spoons wine vinegar	*2 tablespoons wine vinegar*
1 bay leaf	*1 bay leaf*
6 peppercorns	*6 peppercorns*
175 g unsalted or slightly salted butter	*6 oz unsalted or slightly salted butter*
salt	*salt*
white pepper	*white pepper*

Preparation time: about 10 minutes
Cooking time: about 5 minutes

Serve with freshly cooked asparagus, broccoli, warm globe artichokes, or poached, grilled or baked salmon, trout or white fish.

Place the egg yolks in the blender goblet. Put the water, lemon juice, vinegar, bay leaf and peppercorns in a small saucepan and bring to the boil. Boil to reduce to about 1 × 15 ml spoon/1 tablespoon. At the same time melt the butter in another saucepan and heat until it is hot; but do not allow it to brown.
Allow the reduced vinegar mixture to cool slightly, then pour it on to the egg yolks and blend for 3 seconds. With the blender still switched on, remove the centre cap and slowly pour in the hot butter. Replace the cap and continue blending until the sauce is thick. Add salt and pepper to taste. The whole operation should not take longer than 30–40 seconds. Turn the sauce into a serving bowl and serve immediately.

Lemon sauce

Metric	Imperial
300 ml chicken stock	½ pint chicken stock
25 g butter	1 oz butter
25 g plain flour	1 oz plain flour
1 × 1.25 ml spoon grated lemon rind	¼ teaspoon grated lemon rind
1 × 5 ml spoon lemon juice	1 teaspoon lemon juice
salt	salt
freshly ground black pepper	freshly ground black pepper
1 egg yolk	1 egg yolk

Preparation time: about 5 minutes
Cooking time: about 5 minutes

For chicken, turkey, veal and fish.

Place the chicken stock, butter and flour in the blender goblet and blend for a few seconds until the flour is mixed into the stock. Pour into a saucepan and bring slowly to the boil, stirring. Simmer until thickened. Add the lemon rind and juice and salt and pepper to taste. Cool slightly.
Mix a little of the sauce into the egg yolk. Stir the egg yolk mixture into the sauce. Reheat over a very low heat without boiling. Adjust the seasoning, adding more lemon rind or juice to taste.

Variation:
Add 1 × 15 ml spoon/1 tablespoon double cream to the sauce just before serving.

Mint sauce

Metric	Imperial
leaves from 6–8 mint sprigs	leaves from 6–8 mint sprigs
3 × 15 ml spoons boiling water	3 tablespoons boiling water
1 × 15 ml spoon sugar	1 tablespoon sugar
3 × 15 ml spoons vinegar	3 tablespoons vinegar

Preparation time: 5 minutes

Place the mint leaves in the blender goblet. Add the boiling water and blend for about 5 seconds. Add the sugar and vinegar and blend for a further 5–10 seconds or until the mint is finely chopped.
Serves 4–6

From the back: Gooseberry sauce: Mint sauce; Orange rum butter; Lemon sauce

Gooseberry sauce

Metric	Imperial
1 × 425 g can gooseberries	1 × 15 oz can gooseberries
2 × 5 ml spoons cornflour	2 teaspoons cornflour
2 large pinches grated nutmeg	2 large pinches grated nutmeg
25 g butter, chopped	1 oz butter, chopped

Preparation time: about 5 minutes
Cooking time: 5 minutes

Serve with roast or grilled pork, gammon or bacon, roast duck, or grilled, fried or baked mackerel and herrings.

Place the gooseberries and can syrup in the blender goblet. Add the cornflour and nutmeg. Blend until smooth. Pass the purée through a fine strainer into a saucepan to remove pips. Add the butter, and bring slowly to the boil, stirring. Simmer until thickened.
Serves 4–6

Variation:
To use fresh gooseberries instead of canned, cook 225 g/8 oz gooseberries in 150 ml/¼ pint water with sugar to taste, then proceed as above.

Orange rum butter

Metric	Imperial
100 g unsalted butter	4 oz unsalted butter
100 g soft brown sugar	4 oz soft brown sugar
1 × 2.5 ml spoon grated orange rind	½ teaspoon grated orange rind
1 × 1.25 ml spoon ground cinnamon	¼ teaspoon ground cinnamon
3 × 15 ml spoons rum	3 tablespoons rum

Preparation time: 10 minutes

Serve with steamed or baked sponge puddings, pancakes, Christmas pudding, or mince pies.

Place all the ingredients, except the rum, in the mixer bowl or a medium mixing bowl. Using the mixer, beat until light and creamy, about 3–5 minutes. Scrape down the sides of the bowl from time to time, if necessary. Gradually beat in the rum. Place in a covered container in the refrigerator to harden.

Variations:
Use caster sugar instead of brown sugar.
Use brandy instead of rum.
Use lemon rind instead of orange rind and flavour with whisky instead of rum.

Mayonnaise

Metric	Imperial
2 egg yolks, or 1 egg (sizes 1, 2) if blended	2 egg yolks, or 1 large egg if blended
1 × 2.5 ml spoon dry mustard	½ teaspoon dry mustard
1 × 2.5 ml spoon sugar (optional)	½ teaspoon sugar (optional)
1 × 2.5 ml spoon salt	½ teaspoon salt
1 × 1.25 ml spoon pepper	¼ teaspoon pepper
300 ml olive or salad oil	½ pint olive or salad oil
2 × 15 ml spoons wine vinegar or lemon juice	2 tablespoons wine vinegar or lemon juice

Preparation time: about 3 minutes in the blender; about 8 minutes with a mixer

For success all the ingredients must be at room temperature. Take the eggs out of the refrigerator at least 4 hours beforehand.

To make in the blender: place the 2 egg yolks, or 1 whole egg, in the blender goblet. Add the mustard, sugar, if used, and salt and pepper to taste. Blend for a few seconds to combine. With the blender still switched on, remove the centre cap and add half of the oil, very slowly at first and then in a slow steady stream. It should take about 30 seconds. Add half of the vinegar or lemon juice and continue blending until thick. Slowly add the remaining oil followed by the remaining vinegar or lemon juice. Blend until completely mixed. Stop the machine and scrape down the sides of the blender from time to time, if necessary.

To make with a mixer: place the egg yolks in the mixer bowl or a medium mixing bowl. Add the mustard, sugar, if used, and salt and pepper to taste and mix at the highest speed until well combined. Still using the highest speed, add the oil, drop by drop, until the mayonnaise thickens. If the oil is added too quickly at first the mayonnaise will curdle. Once the mayonnaise begins to thicken the oil can be added more quickly, about 1 × 5 ml spoon/1 teaspoon at a time. Always ensure the oil is well beaten in before the next addition. Add half of the vinegar or lemon juice when about half of the oil has been absorbed. When all the oil is mixed in, add the remaining vinegar or lemon juice. Taste and adjust the seasonings, if necessary.
Store the mayonnaise in a tightly covered container in the refrigerator for up to 1 month.
Makes 300 ml/½ pint

Note: if the mayonnaise curdles, pour the curdled mixture into a bowl. Add another egg yolk to the blender or mixing bowl and gradually blend or beat in the curdled mixture, followed by any remaining oil.

Variations:
Curry mayonnaise: add about 1 × 1.25 ml spoon/ ¼ teaspoon mild curry powder, or more to taste, to 150 ml/¼ pint mayonnaise.

Lemon mayonnaise: add about 1 × 1.25 ml spoon/ ¼ teaspoon grated lemon rind to 150 ml/¼ pint mayonnaise.

Horseradish mayonnaise: add 1 × 15 ml spoon/ 1 tablespoon horseradish sauce, or more to taste, to 150 ml/¼ pint mayonnaise.

Garlic mayonnaise: add 1 garlic clove, peeled and finely crushed, to 150 ml/¼ pint mayonnaise. Leave for 2 hours before using.

Tartare sauce: prepare the mayonnaise in the blender goblet. Add 2 × 15 ml spoons/2 tablespoons drained capers, 2 × 15 ml spoons/2 tablespoons roughly chopped gherkins, and 3 large parsley sprigs. Blend until finely chopped and well combined.

Stilton cheese dressing

Metric	Imperial
5 × 15 ml spoons salad oil	5 tablespoons salad oil
2 × 15 ml spoons wine vinegar	2 tablespoons wine vinegar
50 g Stilton cheese, crumbled or roughly chopped	2 oz Stilton cheese, crumbled or roughly chopped
1 × 2.5 ml spoon Dijon mustard	½ teaspoon Dijon mustard
1 × 2.5 ml spoon sugar	½ teaspoon sugar
1 × 1.25 ml spoon salt	¼ teaspoon salt
freshly ground black pepper	freshly ground black pepper

Preparation time: 3 minutes

Use to dress sliced raw button mushrooms, or sliced ripe dessert pears or melon as a starter, or use as a dressing for a mixed green salad or mixed apple, carrot and celery salad.

Place all the ingredients in the blender goblet and blend until smooth and slightly thickened. Adjust the seasoning, if necessary.
Serves 4–6

Variation:
Use 25 g/1 oz blue vein cheese instead of the Stilton.

Basic French dressing

Metric	Imperial
2 × 15 ml spoons wine vinegar	*2 tablespoons wine vinegar*
1 × 5 ml spoon Dijon or French mustard	*1 teaspoon Dijon or French mustard*
salt	*salt*
1 × 1.25 ml spoon freshly ground black pepper	*¼ teaspoon freshly ground black pepper*
5 × 15 ml spoons olive or salad oil	*5 tablespoons olive or salad oil*

Preparation time: about 2 minutes

Use French dressing on all types of salad foods.

Place all the ingredients in the blender goblet and blend for about 10 seconds or until slightly thickened. Serves 4

Note: make up double or treble the quantity using less salt and pepper pro rata and store in a tightly sealed container in the refrigerator for up to 3 weeks. Bring to room temperature before use.

Variations:
Green herb dressing: add 4 large parsley sprigs, 6 chive strands, cut into 5 cm/2 inch lengths, and the leaves from 2 tarragon or basil sprigs with the basic dressing ingredients and blend until the herbs are finely chopped. Only make sufficient for immediate use by adjusting the quantities accordingly.

Garlic dressing: add 1 small garlic clove, peeled and chopped, to the basic dressing ingredients before blending. Alternatively use garlic powder or garlic salt to taste.

Mixed mustard dressing: use half the quantity of Dijon mustard and add 1 × 2.5 ml spoon/½ teaspoon Moutarde de Meaux. Alternatively, use 1 × 5 ml spoon/1 teaspoon tarragon mustard instead of the two mustards.

Curry dressing: add 1 × 1.25 ml spoon/¼ teaspoon mild curry powder to the basic dressing ingredients.

From the left: Basic French dressing; Green herb dressing; Mayonnaise; Stilton cheese dressing

Dark chocolate sauce

Metric	Imperial
50 g plain chocolate	2 oz plain chocolate
150 ml milk or water	¼ pint milk or water
75 g sugar	3 oz sugar
2 × 15 ml spoons cocoa powder	2 tablespoons cocoa powder
25 g butter	1 oz butter
few drops of vanilla essence	few drops of vanilla essence

Preparation time: 5 minutes
Cooking time: about 15 minutes

Serve hot with sponge puddings or ice cream. Serve cold with ice cream, mousses, instant puddings, or canned or poached pears, but stir well before serving cold. Store in a tightly covered container in the refrigerator for up to 1 month.

Break the chocolate into small pieces and drop through the centre of the blender lid on to the revolving blades to chop it. Leave the chocolate in the blender.
Place the milk or water and sugar in a small saucepan and heat gently, stirring, to dissolve the sugar. Do not boil. Pour the milk into the blender goblet, add the cocoa powder and blend until thoroughly mixed. Return to the saucepan, add the butter and bring to the boil, stirring. Turn down the heat and allow to simmer for 10 minutes, stirring occasionally. Add the vanilla essence.
Serves 6

Variations:
Add 1 × 1.25 ml spoon/¼ teaspoon finely grated orange rind instead of the vanilla essence.
Add 1–2 × 15 ml spoons/1–2 tablespoons brandy or rum to the sauce after cooking.
Add 1 × 15 ml spoon/1 tablespoon instant coffee with the cocoa powder.

Soft fruit sauce

Metric	Imperial
225 g soft fruit, e.g. strawberries, raspberries, blackcurrants, blackberries, redcurrants	8 oz soft fruit, e.g. strawberries, raspberries, blackcurrants, blackberries, redcurrants
sugar to taste	sugar to taste

Preparation time: about 5 minutes

Use either one sort of soft fruit or a mixture. Serve cold as a sauce for ice cream, mousses or instant puddings, or stir into plain unsweetened yogurt. Serve hot as a sauce for sponge puddings, milk puddings or pancakes.

Wash and prepare the fruit as necessary. Place the fruit in the blender goblet and blend until a smooth purée. Taste and add sufficient sugar to sweeten. If necessary add a little water or fresh orange or lemon juice to thin down. Pass through a fine nylon strainer to remove the pips.

Plum sauce

Metric	Imperial
225 g ripe plums, halved and stones removed	8 oz ripe plums, halved and stones removed
2 × 15 ml spoons white or brown sugar	2 tablespoons white or brown sugar
3 × 2.5 cm strips orange rind	3 × 1 inch strips orange rind
4 × 15 ml spoons orange juice	4 tablespoons orange juice

Preparation time: about 8 minutes
Cooking time: about 5 minutes

Serve hot as a sauce with sponge puddings, milk puddings and ice cream. Serve cold as a sauce with ice cream, vanilla or lemon mousse and plain unsweetened yogurt.

Place all the ingredients in a medium pan, bring to the boil, cover and simmer for about 5 minutes until cooked. Cool. Remove the pieces of orange rind.
Place the plums and juice in the blender goblet and blend until a smooth purée. Taste and add more sugar, if required, and blend for 5 seconds.
Makes about 250 ml/½ pint sauce

Variations:
Use damsons or greengages instead of plums.
Replace orange juice with red wine or port.

Dark chocolate sauce on pears; Raspberry mousse (see page 31); Soft fruit sauce; Plum sauce at front and on ice cream

TEATIME

The recipes in this chapter have been selected to show the different types of cakes, biscuits and scones which can be prepared with a mixer. Three recipes – Sandwich Cake Mix, Altogether Cake Mix, and Refrigerator Biscuits give larger quantity mixtures which can be divided up and made into different items. When preparation time is short Blender Banana Chocolate Cake is an interesting, quick-to-mix cake.

The mixer will also make icings and cake fillings very quickly to transform a plain Victoria sandwich into something special. A frosting made in the blender takes about 2 minutes to mix and is a perfect topping for cup cakes or larger sponge cakes.

Honey drop scones; Sesame seed loaf

Honey drop scones

Metric	*Imperial*
225 g self-raising flour	*8 oz self-raising flour*
1 × 2.5 ml spoon ground cinnamon	*½ teaspoon ground cinnamon*
50 g caster sugar	*2 oz caster sugar*
1 × 15 ml spoon clear honey	*1 tablespoon clear honey*
1 egg, beaten	*1 egg, beaten*
300 ml milk	*½ pint milk*
oil for cooking	*oil for cooking*

Preparation time: about 8 minutes
Cooking time: 15–20 minutes

Sift the flour, cinnamon and sugar into the mixer bowl or a medium sized mixing bowl. Mix the honey and egg together, using a hand mixer or fork. Pour into the centre of the flour. Using the mixer, gradually beat in the milk until smooth.

Lightly grease a heavy-based frying pan, or griddle, and heat until moderately hot. Drop 15 ml spoonfuls/tablespoonfuls of the mixture on to the pan or griddle, well spaced apart, and cook until bubbles appear on the surface and the underside is golden brown. Turn over and cook the other side until golden brown. Remove the scones from the pan and wrap in a tea towel or kitchen paper to keep warm. Continue making scones until all the batter is used.

Serve warm, spread with butter or cream cheese, and more honey, if wished.

Makes 18–20

Variations:
Flavour with ground mixed spice or 1 × 5 ml spoon/1 teaspoon finely grated lemon rind instead of cinnamon.

Sesame seed loaf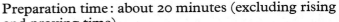

Metric
450 ml tepid milk and
  water, mixed
1 × 15 ml spoon dried
  yeast plus 2 × 5 ml
  spoons sugar, or 25 g
  fresh yeast
750 g strong white flour,
  sifted
2 × 5 ml spoons salt
25 g lard or margarine
beaten egg or milk, to
  glaze
about 1 × 5 ml spoon
  sesame seeds

Imperial
¾ pint tepid milk and
  water, mixed
1 tablespoon dried
  yeast plus 2
  teaspoons sugar, or
  1 oz fresh yeast
1½ lb strong white flour,
  sifted
2 teaspoons salt
1 oz lard or margarine
beaten egg or milk, to
  glaze
about 1 teaspoon
  sesame seeds

Preparation time: about 20 minutes (excluding rising
and proving time)
Cooking time: 45–50 minutes
Oven: 220°C, 425°F, Gas Mark 7

This recipe is only suitable for mixers with dough
kneading attachments. Follow the manufacturer's
instructions for mixing speed.

To prepare the yeast liquid, measure the milk and
water into the mixer bowl. If using dried yeast, stir
it into the liquid with the sugar and leave for 15–20
minutes or until frothy. For fresh yeast, stir it into the
liquid until dissolved and use immediately.
Add the flour, salt and fat, cut into 6–8 pieces, to the
yeast liquid. Fit the dough mixing attachment on to
the mixer. Switch on to a low speed and mix for
about 1 minute or until a dough is formed. Continue
mixing for a further 2–3 minutes to knead the dough.
Turn out the dough on to a lightly floured surface
and knead by hand for about 1 minute until smooth
and elastic.
Return the dough to the washed and dried mixer bowl
and cover with lightly oiled polythene or cling film.
Leave to rise until double its original size. The rising
time varies with the temperature. As a guide, it takes
1 hour in a warm place, 1½–2 hours at room temperature, 4 hours in a cool place, or 12 hours chilled.
Replace the dough mixing attachment on to the mixer
and switch on to a low speed to knock back the dough
for about 1 minute. Turn out the dough on to a
lightly floured surface and divide in half. Press each
half into an oblong the same width as a 450 g/1 lb loaf
tin. Fold each oblong into 3 and turn over so that the
seam is underneath. Smooth over the top and tuck
in the ends. Place in two greased 450 g/1 lb loaf tins.
Brush the tops with beaten egg or milk and sprinkle
with the sesame seeds. Cover the tins loosely with
oiled polythene or cling film and leave in a warm place
to prove until the dough rises to the top of the tin.
This will take about 40 minutes.
Remove the polythene or cling film and bake in a
preheated oven for 30–35 minutes or until the bread
sounds hollow when tapped on the bottom.
Makes 2 × 450 g/1 lb loaves

Variations:
To make a plaited loaf use half the risen dough.
Divide the dough into three equal-sized pieces. Roll
each piece into a strand about 30–35 cm/12–14 inches
long. Pinch together one end of each strand and
plait the strands. Pinch the other ends together. Tuck
both ends underneath and lift onto a greased baking
sheet. Brush with egg or milk and sprinkle with
sesame or poppy seeds or leave plain. Bake as above.
For a slashed top loaf, make diagonal slashes, about
2.5 cm/1 inch apart, on the top of the loaf using a
sharp knife.

Sandwich cake mix

Metric

For the basic 1¾ kg cake mix:

450 g butter or margarine
450 g caster sugar
8 eggs
450 g self-raising flour, sifted

For a lemon cherry sandwich:

500 g prepared basic cake mix
100 g glacé cherries, rinsed, dried, chopped and lightly floured
1 × 5 ml spoon grated lemon rind
Lemon Butter Cream (page 49)

For spiced currant squares:

400 g prepared basic cake mix
50 g currants
25 g self-raising flour
1 × 5 ml spoon ground mixed spice
25 g butter, softened
90 g soft brown sugar

For a marble ring:

500 g prepared basic cake mix
1 × 15 ml spoon cocoa powder
1 × 5 ml spoon milk
50 g icing sugar, sifted
2 × 5 ml spoons hot water
chocolate vermicelli, to decorate

For coffee walnut castles:

350 g prepared basic cake mix
Coffee Butter Cream (page 49)
75 g walnut pieces, chopped in the blender
8–10 walnut halves

Imperial

For the basic 4 lb cake mix:

1 lb butter or margarine
1 lb caster sugar
8 eggs
1 lb self-raising flour, sifted

For a lemon cherry sandwich:

1¼ lb prepared basic cake mix
4 oz glacé cherries, rinsed, dried, chopped and lightly floured
1 teaspoon grated lemon rind
Lemon Butter Cream (page 49)

For spiced currant squares:

14 oz prepared basic cake mix
2 oz currants
1 oz self-raising flour
1 teaspoon ground mixed spice
1 oz butter, softened
3½ oz soft brown sugar

For a marble ring:

1 lb 2 oz prepared basic cake mix
1 tablespoon cocoa powder
1 teaspoon milk
2 oz icing sugar, sifted
2 teaspoons hot water
chocolate vermicelli, to decorate

For coffee walnut castles:

12 oz prepared basic cake mix
Coffee Butter Cream (page 49)
3 oz walnut pieces, chopped in the blender
8–10 walnut halves

Preparation time: about 45 minutes
Cooking time: Lemon cherry sandwich, about 25 minutes
Spiced currant squares, about 30 minutes
Marble ring, about 25 minutes
Coffee walnut castles, about 15 minutes
Oven: 190°C, 375°F, Gas Mark 5

As most domestic ovens are not large enough to bake all the sandwich cake variations at one time, start with the coffee walnut castles which have the shortest cooking time and bake the longest cooking time variation last.

To prepare the basic cake mix, place the butter or margarine and sugar in the mixer bowl or a large mixing bowl. Using the mixer, beat the butter and sugar for about 3 minutes or until light and creamy. Stop the mixer and scrape down the sides of the bowl when necessary. Add the eggs, one at a time, and beat until incorporated before adding the next. Add 1 × 15 ml spoon/1 tablespoon flour with the last egg to prevent curdling. If using a table mixer, fold in the flour using a low speed, or fold it in with a metal spoon. Use the mixture to make the following:

From the left: Lemon cherry sandwich;
Spiced currant squares; Coffee walnut castles; Marble ring

LEMON CHERRY SANDWICH

Weigh the specified amount of prepared basic cake mix and place in a medium mixing bowl. Reserve 2 to 3 whole cherries for decoration and chop the rest. Fold the chopped cherries and lemon rind into the cake mix divide between two greased 20 cm/8 inch sandwich tins. Bake in a preheated oven for about 25 minutes. Turn out on to a wire tray to cool.

Use just under half of the lemon butter cream to sandwich the cake layers together. Spread the remaining butter cream on the top. Decorate with the reserved glacé cherries cut into pieces.

SPICED CURRANT SQUARES

Bottom line and grease an 18 cm/7 inch square baking tin. Weigh the specified amount of the prepared basic cake mix and fold in the currants. Spread evenly in the prepared tin. Place the flour, mixed spice and butter in a small mixing bowl. Use a hand mixer to rub the butter into the flour, or rub in by hand. Stir in the sugar. Sprinkle evenly over the top of the cake mix. Bake in a preheated oven for about 30 minutes. Leave to cool slightly in the tin before removing to a wire tray. Leave to cool completely, then cut into 6 squares.

MARBLE RING

Weigh the specified amount of prepared basic cake mix. Divide in two and place one half in a medium mixing bowl; mix in the cocoa followed by the milk. Place alternate spoonfuls of chocolate and plain cake mix in a greased 1.2 litre/2 pint ring mould and carefully spread evenly. Bake in a preheated oven for about 25 minutes. Cool in the tin for a few minutes before turning out on to a wire tray. Leave to cool. Place the icing sugar in a small basin, add the water and mix to a coating consistency. Spoon the icing over the top of the ring and allow it to run down the sides. Sprinkle with the vermicelli before the icing sets.

COFFEE WALNUT CASTLES

Weigh the specified amount of prepared basic cake mix and divide between 8 to 10 well-greased dariole moulds to fill them by two-thirds. Arrange the moulds on a baking tray. Bake in a preheated oven for about 15 minutes. Turn out of the moulds and leave to cool on a wire tray.

Trim the bases so that the castles stand up straight. Spread the sides of the castles with about three-quarters of the butter cream, then coat the sides with the chopped walnuts. Place the remaining butter cream in a piping bag with large star nozzle and pipe whirls of butter cream on top. Place a walnut half on top of each castle.
Makes 8–10

Soft white frosting

Metric	Imperial
1 egg white	1 egg white
175 g caster sugar	6 oz caster sugar
2 × 5 ml spoons golden syrup	2 teaspoons golden syrup
3 × 15 ml spoons water	3 tablespoons water
1 × 1.25 ml spoon salt	¼ teaspoon salt
1 × 2.5 ml spoon vanilla essence	½ teaspoon vanilla essence

Preparation time: about 15 minutes
Cooking time: about 7 minutes

Enough to cover both the top and sides of a 20 cm/ 8 inch cake.

Place all the ingredients except the vanilla essence in a large heatproof mixing bowl and stand over a pan of fast boiling water. Using a hand mixer and a medium to high speed, beat for about 7 minutes or until the mixture thickens and stands in peaks when the beaters are lifted out. Remove from the heat, add the vanilla essence and continue beating for about 5 minutes or until stiff peaks are formed. Spread over the top and sides of cake with a palette knife for a swirling effect.

Glacé icing

Metric	Imperial
100 g icing sugar, sifted	4 oz icing sugar, sifted
1 × 15 ml spoon hot water	1 tablespoon hot water

Preparation time: 5 minutes

Enough to cover the top of an 18 cm/7 inch cake. (Make up double the quantity to coat the sides as well.)

Place the icing sugar in the mixer bowl or a medium mixing bowl. Using the mixer on the lowest speed, gradually add the water. Continue beating until smooth. Add extra water to thin down the icing or extra icing sugar if a thicker icing is required. Use immediately.

Variations:
Orange or Lemon Glacé Icing: use orange or lemon juice instead of water. Add 1 × 1.25 ml spoon/ ¼ teaspoon finely grated rind, if wished.

Coffee Glacé Icing: Dissolve 1 × 5 ml spoon/1 teaspoon instant coffee powder in the hot water.

Chocolate Glacé Icing: place 50 g/2 oz plain chocolate, a few drops of vanilla essence and the hot water in a small heatproof basin and stand it in a pan of simmering water to melt. Add to the icing sugar.

Butter cream frosting and filling

Metric	Imperial
100 g butter	4 oz butter
175 g icing sugar, sifted	6 oz icing sugar, sifted

Preparation time: about 5 minutes

Enough to fill and cover the top of an 18 cm/7 inch round sandwich cake.

Place the butter in the mixer bowl or a medium mixing bowl. Using the mixer, beat until the butter is creamy. Add half of the icing sugar and beat in, starting on a low speed to prevent the icing sugar flying out of the bowl. Add the remaining icing sugar and beat until light and creamy, about 3 minutes in all. Scrape down the sides of the bowl once or twice during mixing. Flavour and colour as wished.

Variations:
Vanilla Butter Cream: beat in a few drops of vanilla essence.

Coffee Butter Cream: beat in 1 × 15 ml spoon/ 1 tablespoon coffee essence after all the icing sugar has been added. Or add 1 × 15 ml spoon/1 tablespoon instant coffee powder to the icing sugar.

Lemon Butter Cream: beat in 2 × 5 ml spoons/2 teaspoons grated lemon rind and 1 × 15 ml spoon/ 1 tablespoon lemon juice after all the icing sugar has been added.

Orange Butter Cream: beat in 1 × 15 ml spoon/ 1 tablespoon grated orange rind and 1 × 15 ml spoon/ 1 tablespoon orange juice after all the icing sugar has been added.

Nut Butter Cream: add 25 g/1 oz nuts (walnuts, almonds, hazelnuts, brazils), chopped in the blender, after all the icing sugar has been added.

Blender orange frosting

Metric	Imperial
2 × 15 ml spoons orange squash	2 tablespoons orange squash
40 g butter or margarine, softened	1½ oz butter or margarine, softened
175 g icing sugar, sifted	6 oz icing sugar, sifted

Preparation time: about 5 minutes

Enough to fill and cover the top of an 18 cm/7 inch round sandwich cake.

Pour the orange squash into the blender goblet. Add the butter or margarine and then the icing sugar. Blend until well mixed. Stop and scrape down the sides of the goblet from time to time, if necessary.

Variations:
Lemon Frosting: use 2 × 15 ml spoons/2 tablespoons lemon squash instead of orange squash.

Coffee Frosting: use 2 × 15 ml spoons/2 tablespoons coffee essence instead of orange squash.

From the left: Soft white frosting; Glacé icing; Butter cream frosting and filling; Blender orange frosting

Altogether cake mix

Metric
For the basic 1 kg cake mix:
225 g self-raising flour, sifted
2 × 5 ml spoons baking powder
225 g caster sugar
225 g soft (tub) margarine
4 eggs

For St Clement's cup cakes:
450 g prepared basic cake mix
50 g chopped mixed peel
Blender Lemon Frosting (page 49)
crystallized orange or lemon slices, to decorate

For a ginger raisin loaf:
450 g prepared basic cake mix
50 g self-raising flour, sifted
1 × 2.5 ml spoon ground ginger
100 g raisins
2 pieces stem ginger, chopped
1 × 15 ml spoon granulated sugar

Imperial
For the basic 2 lb cake mix:
8 oz self-raising flour, sifted
2 teaspoons baking powder
8 oz caster sugar
8 oz soft (tub) margarine
4 eggs

For St Clement's cup cakes:
1 lb prepared basic cake mix
2 oz chopped mixed peel
Blender Lemon Frosting (page 49)
crystallized orange or lemon slices, to decorate

For a ginger raisin loaf:
1 lb prepared basic cake mix
2 oz self-raising flour, sifted
½ teaspoon ground ginger
4 oz raisins
2 pieces stem ginger, chopped
1 tablespoon granulated sugar

Preparation time: about 30 minutes

Cooking time: St Clement's cup cakes, about 20 minutes
Ginger raisin loaf, about 50–60 minutes
Oven: St Clement's cup cakes, 190°C, 375°F, Gas Mark 5
Ginger raisin loaf, 180°C, 350°F, Gas Mark 4

To prepare the basic cake mix, place all the ingredients in the mixer bowl or a large mixing bowl. Using the mixer, beat for 1 minute until creamy and light. Use the mixture to make the following:

ST CLEMENT'S CUP CAKES
Weigh the specified amount of prepared basic cake mix and fold in the mixed peel. Spoon the mixture into about 22 paper cake cases placed in tartlet tins. Alternatively, divide between 16 greased deep bun tins. Bake in a preheated oven for about 20 minutes. Place the paper cases on a wire tray and leave to cool. Spoon the lemon frosting on top of each cake. Cut each orange or lemon segment into 4 and use to decorate the tops.
Makes about 22

GINGER RAISIN LOAF
Weigh the specified amount of the prepared basic cake mix and fold in all the remaining ingredients, except the sugar. Turn into a greased 450 g (1 lb) loaf tin, spread evenly and sprinkle the top with the sugar. Bake in a preheated oven for 50–60 minutes, or until the cake begins to pull away from the sides of the tin. Turn out on to a wire tray and leave to cool.

Variations:
St Clement's cup cakes: add 50 g/2 oz chocolate chips to the basic cake mixture instead of the chopped mixed peel. Ice with Blender Orange Frosting, or Coffee Frosting (page 49).

Ginger raisin loaf: omit the ground ginger and stem ginger; flavour with ground cinnamon or mixed spice and add 25 g/1 oz chopped walnuts.
Use mixed dried fruit or stoned chopped dates instead of raisins.

Ginger raisin loaf; St Clement's cup cakes

Refrigerator biscuits

Metric	Imperial
450 g plain flour	1 lb plain flour
2 × 5 ml spoons baking powder	2 teaspoons baking powder
225 g butter	8 oz butter
350 g caster sugar	12 oz caster sugar
2 eggs, beaten	2 eggs, beaten

Preparation time: about 20 minutes
Cooking time: about 20 minutes
Oven: 190°C, 375°F, Gas Mark 5

As a general guide to yields, the complete mix makes about 90 biscuits. A quarter of the mix will make 22–24 biscuits.

Sift the flour and baking powder into the mixer bowl or a large mixing bowl. Cut the butter into 1 cm/½ inch cubes and add to the flour. Using the mixer, rub the butter into the flour until the mixture resembles fine breadcrumbs. Mix in the sugar. Continue mixing and add the eggs to form a soft dough. Cut off the quantity required for immediate use, wrap in foil or cling film and leave to rest in the refrigerator for 30 minutes. Cut the remaining dough into convenient sized pieces, roll into sausage shapes, wrap tightly in foil and place in the freezer.
Roll out the rested dough thinly and cut into shapes, e.g. 5 cm/2 in squares, using a knife, or rounds, using a plain or fluted cutter, 7.5 × 2.5 cm/3 × 1 inch fingers, or other fancy shapes. Place on baking sheets, allowing space for the biscuits to spread slightly. Bake in a pre-heated oven for 15–20 minutes or until crisp and lightly browned. Cool on a wire tray.
To use the frozen mix, leave to thaw completely, then roll out, cut into shapes and bake as above. Alternatively, thaw the dough rolls until just beginning to soften and cut into 3 mm/⅛ inch thick slices while still firm. Bake as above.
The biscuits can be decorated as follows:

Before baking: with halved or quartered glacé cherries;
sprinkled with a few chocolate chips;
sprinkled with chopped walnuts or almonds.

After baking: sandwiched together with jam, lemon curd or Butter Cream (page 49);
iced with Glacé Icing (page 48) and decorated with chopped nuts or halved or quartered glacé cherries.

Variations:
Spice biscuits: sift 4 × 5 ml spoons/4 teaspoons ground mixed spice with the flour.

Orange or lemon biscuits: add 4 × 5 ml spoons/4 teaspoons grated lemon or orange rind to the flour.

Currant biscuits: add 100 g/4 oz currants to the rubbed-in mixture.

Almond biscuits: add 1 × 5 ml spoon/1 teaspoon almond essence with the egg.

Refrigerator biscuits; Blender banana chocolate cake

Blender banana chocolate cake

Metric	Imperial
225 g self-raising flour	*8 oz self-raising flour*
1 × 2.5 ml spoon baking powder	*½ teaspoon baking powder*
40 g drinking chocolate	*1½ oz drinking chocolate*
2 eggs	*2 eggs*
4 × 15 ml spoons milk	*4 tablespoons milk*
150 g caster sugar	*5 oz caster sugar*
100 g soft (tub) margarine	*4 oz soft (tub) margarine*
2 small ripe bananas, cut into 5 cm pieces	*2 small ripe bananas, cut into 2 inch pieces*

Preparation time: about 10 minutes
Cooking time: 1 hour
Oven: 180°C, 350°F, Gas Mark 4

This is best kept for 1 day before serving; by then it will be a deliciously moist close-textured cake.

Sift the flour, baking powder and chocolate powder into a large mixing bowl. Place all the other ingredients in the blender goblet in the order given. Blend for about 20 seconds on a high speed. The mixture will look curdled. Pour into the dry ingredients in the bowl and mix together by hand.

Turn into a greased 18 cm/7 inch round cake tin. Bake in a preheated oven for about 1 hour or until cooked in the centre: test with a skewer. Turn out on to a wire tray and leave to cool.

BABY FOODS

The blender makes it simple to convert cooked meat, chicken, liver and vegetables into a smooth purée when you start introducing solid foods to your baby. For toddlers the food can be processed for a shorter time to keep a coarser texture.

When you are taking food from family dishes to use for the baby, remember that babies like bland, unseasoned food, so add salt and other strongly flavoured seasonings after the baby's food has been removed.

Toddlers will enjoy savoury sandwich fillings based on meat and cheese; this is a good way of introducing extra protein into their diet, especially on days when they find it difficult to eat up all the main meal.

As hygiene is most important in all aspects of caring for babies, it is always wise to thoroughly rinse the blender goblet in hot water before starting to prepare food.

Vegetable purées

The blender is excellent for reducing cooked vegetables to smooth purées to serve as part of the baby's main meal or to add to cooked meat or fish when preparing a puréed main meal.

The minimum amount which can be puréed depends on the size of the blender goblet. Remember that to purée efficiently the blades should be covered. Surplus purée can be frozen in one-meal portions for future use and should be frozen in small plastic containers or ice cube trays.

Vegetables such as broccoli, carrot, cabbage, cauliflower, celery, courgette, green beans, marrow, parsnip, peas, spinach, sprouts, swede and turnip can all be puréed.

To make a purée, cook the prepared vegetables in the minimum amount of boiling water, without salt, until just tender. Drain the vegetables, reserving the liquor. Place the cooked vegetables in the blender goblet just to cover the blades or, to prepare the maximum quantity fill the goblet up to one-third full. Add up to 3–4 × 15 ml spoons/3–4 tablespoons of the cooking liquor and blend until a smooth purée. Stop the machine and scrape down the sides of the goblet from time to time, if necessary. Add extra liquor or water to make into the correct consistency.

Roast meat dinner

Metric
50 g cooked lean roast
  beef, lamb, veal,
  chicken or turkey
1 small portion of cooked
  vegetable (1 medium
  carrot, 4–5 Brussels
  sprouts, 2–3 cauliflower
  florets, 3–4 × 15 ml
  spoons cooked peas or
  sliced green beans)
3–4 × 15 ml spoons
  unseasoned meat juice
  or stock

Imperial
2 oz cooked lean roast
  beef, lamb, veal,
  chicken or turkey
1 small portion of cooked
  vegetable (1 medium
  carrot, 4–5 Brussels
  sprouts, 2–3 cauliflower
  florets, 3–4 table-
  spoons cooked peas or
  sliced green beans)
3–4 tablespoons
  unseasoned meat juice
  or stock

Preparation time: about 5 minutes

Cut the meat and vegetables, if necessary, into 1 cm/
½ inch pieces. Place in the blender goblet with
3 × 15 ml spoons/3 tablespoons meat juice or stock.
Blend until finely chopped or a smooth purée. It may
be necessary to stop the machine and scrape down the
sides of the goblet once or twice until the mixture
begins to purée. Add extra meat juice or stock to make
the right consistency for the baby. Reheat to serve.
Serves 1

Chicken risotto

Metric
1 small chicken breast
few drops of vegetable oil
2 × 15 ml spoons cooked
  rice
1 egg yolk
2 cauliflower florets,
  cooked
3–4 × 15 ml spoons
  unseasoned chicken
  stock or water

Imperial
1 small chicken breast
few drops of vegetable oil
2 tablespoons cooked
  rice
1 egg yolk
2 cauliflower florets,
  cooked
3–4 tablespoons
  unseasoned chicken
  stock or water

Preparation time: about 10 minutes
Cooking time: about 15 minutes

Smear the chicken breast very lightly with the
vegetable oil and place under a moderately hot grill.
Cook for about 8 minutes. Turn over and grill the
other side for a further 5 minutes or until cooked.
Remove the meat from the bone and cut into 1 cm/
½ inch pieces.
Place the chicken, rice, egg yolk, cauliflower and
3 × 15 ml spoons/3 tablespoons of the stock or water
in the blender goblet. Blend until finely chopped or a
smooth purée. It may be necessary to stop the
machine and scrape down the sides of the goblet
once or twice until the mixture begins to purée. Add
more stock or water to make into the correct consistency for the baby. Reheat to serve.
Serves 1–2

Variations:
Use 1 small cooked carrot or 3 × 15 ml spoons/3
tablespoons cooked peas instead of the cauliflower.
Omit the rice.

Vegetable purée; Roast meat dinner; Chicken risotto

Liver, carrot and tomato

Metric	Imperial
50–75 g liver	2–3 oz liver
2 medium tomatoes, skinned, seeded and chopped	2 medium tomatoes, skinned, seeded and chopped
1 × 15 ml spoon water	1 tablespoon water
1 small carrot, peeled, cooked and chopped	1 small carrot, peeled, cooked and chopped
about 1 × 5 ml spoon baby rice	about 1 teaspoon baby rice

Preparation time: about 8 minutes
Cooking time: about 10 minutes

Cut away any connective tissue from the liver. Wash and dry the liver and slice thinly. Place the liver, tomatoes and water in a small pan and slowly bring to the boil. Cover the pan and cook very gently for about 10 minutes or until the liver is tender.
Place the liver, cooking liquor and carrot in the blender goblet and blend until smooth. Turn into a small pan and reheat. Add sufficient baby rice to thicken to the correct consistency for the baby.
Serves 1

Cheesy fish dinner

Metric	Imperial
50–75 g plaice, haddock, cod or other white fish, fillet, fresh or frozen	2–3 oz plaice, haddock, cod or other white fish fillet, fresh or frozen
2 × 15 ml spoons water or milk	2 tablespoons water or milk
1 small potato, peeled and cooked	1 small potato, peeled and cooked
2 × 5 ml spoons finely grated or chopped mild Cheddar cheese	2 teaspoons finely grated or chopped mild Cheddar cheese

Preparation time: about 10 minutes
Cooking time: 15–20 minutes

Put the fish on a heatproof plate with the water or milk and cover with foil. Place over a pan of simmering water and steam for 15–20 minutes or until cooked. Flake the fish, removing the skin and any stray bones. Place the fish, cooking liquor, potato and cheese in the blender goblet and blend until puréed. Stop the machine and scrape down the sides of the goblet once or twice and add extra water or milk if necessary. Reheat and serve with puréed carrot, spinach or peas.
Serves 1

Tomato purée

Tomatoes can be puréed raw or cooked. Always skin them and remove all the seeds before puréeing. It should not be necessary to add water. Use the tomato purée to moisten cooked meat, chicken, liver and fish when preparing puréed main meals, and to add to soups and sandwich fillings.

Beef casserole and vegetables

Metric	Imperial
50 g cooked lean beef from the casserole	2 oz cooked lean beef from the casserole
1 small cooked carrot from the casserole	1 small cooked carrot from the casserole
1 small cooked celery stick from the casserole	1 small cooked celery stick from the casserole
3–4 × 15 ml spoons unseasoned casserole gravy	3–4 tablespoons unseasoned casserole gravy

Preparation time: about 5 minutes

This recipe can be used as a basic guide for preparing a meal from lamb, chicken or veal casseroles. If the vegetables in the casserole are unsuitable for babies, cook carrot, swede, celery or peas separately and add to the meat in the blender.

Cut up the beef, carrot and celery roughly into 1 cm/½ inch pieces and place in the blender goblet with 3 × 15 ml spoons/3 tablespoons of the casserole gravy. Blend until finely chopped or a smooth purée. It may be necessary to stop the machine and scrape down the sides of the goblet once or twice until the mixture begins to purée. Add extra gravy to make into the correct consistency for the baby. Reheat to serve. Serve with a green vegetable purée.
Serves 1

From the front: Liver, carrot and tomato; Tomato purée; Cheesy fish dinner; Beef casserole and vegetables

Fruit purées

Cooked and raw fruits can be puréed in the blender in a similar way to vegetables. Add fruit purées to milk puddings, egg custard and plain unsweetened yogurt, or serve with ice cream. For cooked fruit purées use apples, fresh apricots, blackcurrants, pears and plums. Cook the prepared fruit in the minimum amount of water without sugar until just tender. Drain the fruit, reserving the cooking liquor. Place the cooked fruit in the blender goblet just to cover the blades or, to prepare the maximum quantity, fill the goblet to one-third full. Add up to 3–4 × 15 ml spoons/3–4 tablespoons of the cooking liquor and blend until smooth. Stop the machine and scrape down the sides of the goblet from time to time if necessary. Add extra liquor or water to make into the correct consistency. Dried apricots and prunes can be prepared by this method. Soak them in water overnight before cooking. For fresh raw fruit purées use bananas, grapes, grapefruits, oranges, melon, ripe peaches, plums and pears. Remove all peel, pips and stones before puréeing. For grapefruit and oranges, cut off the peel and all the white pith and cut either side of each segment to remove the membrane and centre pithy core. Remove all the pips from the segments. Place the prepared fruit in the blender goblet, without extra liquid, and blend until smooth.

Banana yogurt pudding

Metric	*Imperial*
3 × 15 ml spoons plain unsweetened yogurt	*3 tablespoons plain unsweetened yogurt*
½ banana, sliced	*½ banana, sliced*
2 × 5 ml spoons baby cereal	*2 teaspoons baby cereal*

Preparation time: 5 minutes

Place all the ingredients in the blender goblet and blend until a smooth purée. Add extra cereal to make thicker, if wished.
Serves 1

Variations:
Use 1 small ripe pear, peeled and cored, or 1 fresh ripe peach, peeled and stoned, instead of banana.

Apple with rice

Metric
3 × 15 ml spoons home-
    made rice pudding
4 × 15 ml spoons cooked
    apples

Imperial
3 tablespoons home-
    made rice pudding
4 tablespoons cooked
    apples

Preparation time: 5 minutes

Place both ingredients in the blender goblet and blend
until smooth.
Serves 1

Variations:
Use 4–6 cooked prunes, stoned, or cooked dried
apricots instead of apples.

From the left: Fruit purée; Banana yogurt pudding;
Apple with rice; Prune custard

Prune custard

Metric
1 egg yolk
1 × 2.5 ml spoon sugar
6 × 15 ml spoons milk
6 cooked prunes, stoned

Imperial
1 egg yolk
½ teaspoon sugar
6 tablespoons milk
6 cooked prunes, stoned

Preparation time: about 12 minutes

Mix the egg yolk and sugar together in a small heatproof basin and add the milk. Place over a pan of
simmering water and stir until the custard thickens.
Remove the basin from the heat and pour the custard
into the blender goblet. Add the prunes and blend
until smooth.
Serves 1

Variations:
Use 3 × 15 ml spoons/3 tablespoons cooked apples, 4
cooked dried apricots, 4 cooked plums, stoned, ½
banana or 1 fresh ripe peach, peeled and stoned,
instead of the prunes.

Sandwich fillings
Savoury ham

Metric
50 g cooked lean ham
1 × 15 ml spoon plain
  unsweetened yogurt
15 g butter, melted

Imperial
2 oz cooked lean ham
1 tablespoon plain
  unsweetened yogurt
½ oz butter, melted

Preparation time: 5 minutes

Cut the ham into 1 cm/½ inch pieces and place in the blender goblet with the yogurt and melted butter. Blend until a smooth paste is formed. Stop the machine and scrape down the sides of the goblet two or three times. Add extra yogurt, if necessary.
Spreads 2 large bread slices

Variations:
Use cooked chicken meat instead of ham.
Replace half of the ham with cooked liver or cooked chicken meat.

Cheese and tomato

Metric
50 g mild Cheddar cheese,
  roughly chopped
1 tomato, skinned,
  seeded and chopped
1 × 15 ml spoon boiling
  water

Imperial
2 oz mild Cheddar cheese,
  roughly chopped
1 tomato, skinned,
  seeded and chopped
1 tablespoon boiling
  water

Preparation time: about 6 minutes (excluding chilling time)

Drop the cheese into the blender goblet through the centre of the lid on to the revolving blades. When it is finely chopped, add the tomato and blend for a few seconds to purée. Add the boiling water and blend until smooth. Stop the machine and scrape down the sides of the goblet from time to time, if necessary. Turn out of the blender and chill for 30 minutes to thicken. Any unused filling can be stored in the refrigerator for up to two days.
Spreads 2 large bread slices

Creamed egg

Metric
50 g full fat soft cheese
2 × 5 ml spoons milk
1 hard-boiled egg, finely
    chopped

Imperial
2 oz full fat soft cheese
2 teaspoons milk
1 hard-boiled egg, finely
    chopped

Preparation time: about 5 minutes

Place the cheese in a bowl. Using a hand mixer, beat until smooth. Beat in the milk one spoon at a time. Add the egg and beat until incorporated. Add a little extra milk if too stiff.
Spreads 2–3 large bread slices

Variations:
Use sieved raw tomato purée instead of milk for under 12-month-old babies. Tomato ketchup can be used for older babies, if liked.
Spread the bread very thinly with yeast extract before adding the creamed egg filling.

Chocolate and honey; Cheese and tomato;
Creamed egg; Savoury ham

Chocolate and honey

Metric
100 g cottage cheese
1 × 5 ml spoon cocoa
    powder
2 × 5 ml spoons clear
    honey

Imperial
4 oz cottage cheese
1 teaspoon cocoa
    powder
2 teaspoons clear
    honey

Preparation time: about 4 minutes

Place the cottage cheese in the blender goblet, add the cocoa powder and then the honey. Blend until almost smooth and the cocoa is mixed in. Stop the machine and scrape down the sides of the goblet, if necessary. Store any unused mixture in the refrigerator for up to two days.
Spreads 2–3 large bread slices

Variation:
Omit cocoa powder and add 1–2 × 15 ml spoons/1–2 tablespoons thick apricot purée, made from dried apricots to the cottage cheese.

DRINKS

Drinks of all types are quickly prepared in the blender. Many kinds of fruit can be used for flavouring. Fresh fruit, of course, gives the best flavour, but fruit from the freezer or canned fruit may be used. Drinks made from fruit with small pips will need to be strained. For citrus fruits it is necessary to remove the rind and pith which give a better taste but a few slivers of rind can be added, if liked.

Let children make their own milk shakes and ice cream sodas. Bananas and strawberries can be particularly delicious in milk shakes.

Cocktails are becoming increasingly popular, and the blender is particularly good for ones calling for egg yolks or whites which make the drink very smooth and creamy. Drinks using egg whites should not be made in a smaller quantity than given in the recipe.

To obtain the correct balance of ingredients in a drink made with alcohol use the same measure for all ingredients.

The capacity of the measure used in the following drinks is about 4 × 15 ml spoons/4 tablespoons. A smaller or larger measure can be used, depending on individual taste and the quantity required.

In some of the larger powerful blenders ice cubes may be added with the other ingredients to chill the drink. Before adding any ice cubes to a drink, check with the manufacturer's instructions to find out if they can be chopped in your blender.

Vitality drink

Metric	*Imperial*
1 large dessert apple, cored and cut into 1 cm thick pieces	*1 large dessert apple, cored and cut into ½ inch thick pieces*
1 large carrot, scrubbed and cut into 1 cm thick slices	*1 large carrot, scrubbed and cut into ½ inch thick slices*
1 small celery stick, cut into 2.5 cm lengths	*1 small celery stick, cut into 1 inch lengths*
1 × 5 mm thick lemon slice, cut into 4	*1 × ¼ inch thick lemon slice, cut into 4*
2 small parsley sprigs	*2 small parsley sprigs*
2 × 5 ml spoons honey	*2 teaspoons honey*
600 ml water	*1 pint water*

Preparation time: about 10 minutes

Apples with a 'tart' taste, such as Granny Smith's, give the best flavour. Alternatively, use a small cooking apple and increase the honey, if wished.

Place all the ingredients in the blender goblet and blend for about 20 seconds. Strain into a jug and chill.
Serves 4

From the left: Vitality drink; Breakfast in a glass; Blender citrus drink

216, Bencombe Road, Purley, Surrey

Breakfast in a glass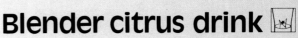

Metric
150 ml orange juice,
  chilled
1 egg
150 ml plain unsweetened
  yogurt

Imperial
¼ pint orange juice,
  chilled
1 egg
¼ pint plain unsweetened
  yogurt

Preparation time: 3 minutes

Place all the ingredients in the blender goblet and blend for 5–10 seconds. Serve immediately.
Serves 1

Variations:
Use grapefruit juice instead of orange juice.
Omit the egg, if wished.
Add honey or sugar to taste, if wished.
Add 1 × 15 ml spoon/1 tablespoon powdered skimmed milk to the ingredients.

Blender citrus drink

Metric
3 × 2.5 cm strips orange
  rind (no pith)
3 medium oranges, peeled
  and pith removed
2 × 5 mm thick lemon
  slices
3 × 15 ml spoons sugar
900 ml water
2 orange slices, to
  decorate

Imperial
3 × 1 inch strips orange
  rind (no pith)
3 medium oranges, peeled
  and pith removed
2 × ¼ inch thick lemon
  slices
3 tablespoons sugar
1½ pints water
2 orange slices, to
  decorate

Preparation time: about 8 minutes

Place the orange rind strips in the blender goblet. Cut each orange into 8 pieces and each lemon slice into 4. Place in the blender goblet with the sugar and 600 ml/1 pint of the water. Blend for 20 seconds. Strain into a jug and add the remaining 300 ml/ ½ pint water. Chill.
To serve, stir and float orange slices on top.
Serves 4–6

Variations:
Use 2 small grapefruit instead of oranges or a mixture of grapefruit and orange.

Strawberry milk shake

Metric	Imperial
300 ml milk, chilled	½ pint milk, chilled
100 g fresh or frozen strawberries, hulled	4 oz fresh or frozen strawberries, hulled
1 × 15 ml spoon caster sugar	1 tablespoon caster sugar

Preparation time: 3 minutes

Place all the ingredients in the blender goblet and blend for 10–15 seconds. Strain into tall glasses and serve immediately.
Serves 1–2

Variations:
Use 4 × 15 ml spoons/4 tablespoons drained canned strawberries instead of fresh or frozen strawberries.
Use fresh, frozen or canned raspberries instead of strawberries. Pour through a fine nylon strainer to remove the pips before serving.
Use 4 × 15 ml spoons/4 tablespoons crushed pineapple or 3 pineapple rings, chopped, instead of strawberries.
Use 2 × 15 ml spoons/2 tablespoons coffee essence instead of strawberries. Add sugar to taste.
Use 4–5 × 15 ml spoons/4–5 tablespoons drained fresh or canned fruit salad instead of strawberries.

Banana yogurt shake

Metric	Imperial
300 ml milk, chilled	½ pint milk, chilled
1 large ripe banana	1 large ripe banana
150 ml hazelnut yogurt, chilled	¼ pint hazelnut yogurt, chilled
1 × 15 ml spoon sugar	1 tablespoon sugar

Preparation time: 3 minutes

Place all the ingredients in the blender goblet and blend for 10–15 seconds until smooth. Pour into tall glasses and serve immediately.
Serves 1–2

Variations:
Use plain unsweetened mandarin, strawberry or lemon flavoured yogurt instead of hazelnut yogurt.
Use 6 apricot halves instead of the banana.
Use 2–3 pineapple rings, roughly chopped, instead of the banana.

Blackcurrant soda

Metric	Imperial
150 ml milk, chilled	¼ pint milk, chilled
2 × 15 ml spoons blackcurrant syrup	2 tablespoons blackcurrant syrup
4 × 15 ml spoons vanilla ice cream	4 tablespoons vanilla ice cream
about 150 ml soda water	about ¼ pint soda water

Preparation time: 3 minutes

Place all the ingredients, except the soda water, in the blender goblet. Blend for about 10 seconds. Pour into tall glasses and top up with soda water. Serve immediately.
Serves 1–2

Variations:
Use 6 canned apricot halves instead of the blackcurrant syrup.
Use 100 g/4 oz fresh or frozen raspberries, strawberries or blackberries instead of blackcurrant syrup. Strain before serving.

Nectar

Metric	Imperial
300 ml orange juice, chilled	½ pint orange juice, chilled
8 canned apricot halves	8 canned apricot halves
1 × 15 ml spoon lemon juice	1 tablespoon lemon juice
1 × 15 ml spoon honey	1 tablespoon honey

Preparation time: 5 minutes

Place all the ingredients in the blender goblet and blend for 10–15 seconds. Chill well before serving.
Serves 2–3

Variation:
Use 8 canned peach slices instead of apricot halves.

From the left: Banana yogurt shake; Strawberry milk shake; Nectar; Blackcurrant soda

Brandy booster

Metric	Imperial
1 measure brandy	*1 measure brandy*
1 measure fresh orange juice	*1 measure fresh orange juice*
½ measure fresh lemon juice	*½ measure fresh lemon juice*
1 egg yolk	*1 egg yolk*
1 × 2.5 ml spoon icing sugar	*½ teaspoon icing sugar*
crushed ice	*crushed ice*

Preparation time: 5 minutes

Place all the ingredients in the blender goblet and blend for 5–10 seconds. Serve immediately.
Serves 1

From the left: Brandy booster; Night-time nog; Chocolate cooler; Iced coffee special

Night-time nog

Metric	Imperial
150 ml milk	*¼ pint milk*
1 × 15 ml spoon sugar	*1 tablespoon sugar*
1 measure whisky, brandy, rum or sherry	*1 measure whisky, brandy, rum or sherry*
1 egg	*1 egg*
grated nutmeg, for sprinkling	*grated nutmeg, for sprinkling*

Preparation time: 5 minutes

Heat the milk to just under boiling point. Pour into the blender goblet and add the sugar, whisky, or alcohol of choice, and egg. Blend for 10 seconds. Pour into a heatproof glass and sprinkle the top with a little nutmeg. Serve immediately.
Serves 1

Chocolate cooler

Metric	*Imperial*
300 ml milk, chilled	½ pint milk, chilled
4 × 5 ml spoons drinking chocolate	4 teaspoons drinking chocolate
1 × 5 ml spoon sugar (optional)	1 teaspoon sugar (optional)
4 × 15 ml spoons vanilla ice cream	4 tablespoons vanilla ice cream
a little drinking chocolate, for sprinkling	a little drinking chocolate, for sprinkling

Preparation time: 3 minutes

Place all the ingredients in the blender goblet and blend for about 10 seconds. Pour into tall glasses and sprinkle a little chocolate powder on top. Serve immediately.
Serves 1–2

Variations:
Use coffee ice cream instead of vanilla ice cream.
Add 1 × 5 ml spoon/1 teaspoon instant coffee powder or coffee essence.
Add a few drops of peppermint essence.

Iced coffee special

Metric	*Imperial*
1 × 15 ml spoon instant coffee powder	1 tablespoon instant coffee powder
2 × 15 ml spoons boiling water	2 tablespoons boiling water
300 ml milk, chilled	½ pint milk, chilled
4 × 15 ml spoons vanilla ice cream	4 tablespoons vanilla ice cream
1 × 15 ml spoon sugar (optional)	1 tablespoon sugar (optional)
2 × 15 ml spoons brandy ground cinnamon, for sprinkling	2 tablespoons brandy ground cinnamon, for sprinkling

Preparation time: about 5 minutes (excluding cooling time)

Dissolve the coffee in the boiling water and leave to go cold.
Place all the ingredients, except the cinnamon, in the blender goblet and blend for about 10 seconds. Pour into tall glasses and sprinkle the top with a little cinnamon.
Serves 1–2

Tomato and orange cocktail

Metric
600 ml tomato juice, chilled
2 medium oranges, peeled and cut into 8 pieces
1 × 10 cm piece cucumber, cut into 8 pieces
1 × 2.5 ml spoon Worcestershire sauce
salt
orange and cucumber slices, to garnish

Imperial
1 pint tomato juice, chilled
2 medium oranges, peeled and cut into 8 pieces
1 × 4 inch piece cucumber, cut into 8 pieces
½ teaspoon Worcestershire sauce
salt
orange and cucumber slices, to garnish

Preparation time: about 7 minutes

Place all the ingredients in the blender goblet and blend for 10–15 seconds. Adjust the seasoning, adding extra Worcestershire sauce and salt to taste. Strain into a jug. Chill.
To serve, stir well and float orange and cucumber slices on top, or arrange on the side of the glass.
Serves 4

Variations:
Use 150 ml/¼ pint fresh orange juice instead of whole oranges.
Add vodka, to taste.

Sherry flip

Metric
1 measure medium sweet or sweet sherry
1 × 5 ml spoon icing sugar
1 egg

Imperial
1 measure medium sweet or sweet sherry
1 teaspoon icing sugar
1 egg

Preparation time: 3 minutes

Place all the ingredients in the blender goblet and blend for about 5 seconds. Pour into a glass and serve immediately.
Serves 1

Variations:
Add extra or less sugar to taste.
Use brandy, whisky or rum instead of sherry.

Fair lady cocktail

Metric
1 egg white
powdered sugar (page 7)
2 measures gin
6 measures grapefruit juice, chilled
dash of Cointreau
crushed ice

Imperial
1 egg white
powdered sugar (page 7)
2 measures gin
6 measures grapefruit juice, chilled
dash of Cointreau
crushed ice

Preparation time: 5 minutes

Dip the edges of two or three glasses in the egg white and then in the sugar to frost them.
Place the remaining egg white, the gin, grapefruit juice, Cointreau and a little crushed ice in the blender goblet and blend for 5–10 seconds. Pour into glasses and serve immediately.
Serves 2–3

Variations:
Use orange juice instead of grapefruit juice or use a mixture of orange and grapefruit juice.
Use vodka instead of gin.

Golden shot

Metric
1 measure whisky
3 measures orange juice, chilled
1 egg yolk
crushed ice

Imperial
1 measure whisky
3 measures orange juice, chilled
1 egg yolk
crushed ice

Preparation time: 3 minutes

Place all the ingredients in the blender goblet and blend for 5–10 seconds. Pour into glasses and serve immediately.
Serves 1–2

Variation:
Use brandy or rum instead of whisky.

From the front, clockwise: Golden shot; Sherry flip; Tomato and orange cocktail; Fair lady cocktail

PARTY FARE

Dips and spreads, pâtés and pizzas are all quickly made in a mixer or blender. Cooked meats, liver and vegetables can be reduced to thick purées in the blender. Some form of liquid, such as melted butter, lemon juice, stock or cream, usually needs to be added. The amount of liquid, which can often be taken from the recipe, will depend on the texture of the food. Do not fill the goblet more than about one-third full, but always remember to cover the blades.

Divide the ingredients into batches using some of each ingredient. At the start it will be necessary to switch off the motor and scrape the food on to the centre of the blades several times before it begins to purée efficiently. If the food stops moving in the goblet, switch off and scrape down. It is a waste of time to continue as an air pocket will have formed between the blades and the food. If the mixture looks too stiff add a little extra liquid. Party puddings such as meringues become simple and speedier to make too.

Cheese and paprika dip

Metric	Imperial
225 g full fat soft cheese	*8 oz full fat soft cheese*
4 × 15 ml spoons soured cream or plain unsweetened yogurt	*4 tablespoons soured cream or plain unsweetened yogurt*
1 × 5 ml spoon tomato purée	*1 teaspoon tomato purée*
1 × 2.5 ml spoon paprika	*½ teaspoon paprika*
salt	*salt*
pepper	*pepper*
4 spring onions, finely chopped	*4 spring onions, finely chopped*
1 small green pepper, cored, seeded and finely chopped	*1 small green pepper, cored, seeded and finely chopped*
3 stuffed green olives, finely chopped	*3 stuffed green olives, finely chopped*

Preparation time: about 10 minutes (excluding chilling time)

Place the cheese, soured cream or yogurt, tomato purée, paprika, and salt and pepper to taste, in the mixing bowl. Using the mixer, beat until smooth and creamy. Add the remaining ingredients and beat until combined. Turn into a serving bowl. Cover with cling film or foil and chill in the refrigerator for at least 4 hours before serving.
Serves 8–10

Cheese and paprika dip; Olive and tuna spread; Mixed fish pâté

Olive and tuna spread

Metric

1 × 200 g can tuna in oil
1 × 15 ml spoon lemon
  juice
10 stuffed green olives
1 × 15 ml spoon capers
3 spring onions, cut into
  2.5 cm lengths
freshly ground black
  pepper

Imperial

1 × 7 oz can tuna in oil
1 tablespoon lemon
  juice
10 stuffed green olives
1 tablespoon capers
3 spring onions, cut into
  1 inch lengths
freshly ground black
  pepper

Preparation time: 10 minutes (excluding resting time)

Place all the ingredients in the blender goblet, including the oil from the canned tuna. Blend until a smooth purée. Stop the machine from time to time to scrape the mixture on to the blades, if necessary. Adjust the seasoning. Turn out, cover and leave for 2 hours before using.
Use to spread on small plain biscuits as a base for canapés. Top with a slice of hard-boiled egg, or a strip of red pepper, or slices of stuffed green olive, or rolled anchovy fillets. Alternatively, use to fill small short-crust pastry cases and garnish as above.
Spreads 20–30 small biscuits

Variation:
Use stoned black olives instead of stuffed green olives.

Mixed fish pâté

Metric

225 g cod fillets, skinned
  and cut into 2.5 cm
  pieces
225 g smoked haddock
  fillets, skinned
100 g butter
2 × 15 ml spoons plain
  flour
salt
freshly ground black
  pepper
2 eggs, beaten
150 ml single cream

Imperial

8 oz cod fillets, skinned
  and cut into 1 inch
  pieces
8 oz smoked haddock
  fillets, skinned
4 oz butter
2 tablespoons plain
  flour
salt
freshly ground black
  pepper
2 eggs, beaten
¼ pint single cream

Preparation time: 25 minutes
Cooking time: about 50 minutes
Oven: 160°C, 325°F, Gas Mark 3

Place half the fish in the blender goblet and blend until puréed. It will be necessary to stop the machine and move the fish back on to the blades several times before the fish is evenly puréed. Repeat with the other half of the fish.
Place the butter in the mixer bowl, or a medium sized mixing bowl. Using the mixer, beat the butter until creamy. Add the flour and beat in. Gradually add the fish, beating well between each addition. Beat in salt and pepper to taste. Gradually add the eggs, beating well. Finally, gradually beat in the cream.
Place the mixture in a well-buttered 1.2 litre/2 pint terrine or soufflé dish. Cover with a lid or foil and place in a roasting tin of warm water. Place in a preheated oven and cook for about 50 minutes, or until just set.
Leave to cool until just warm before turning out of the dish. Cover with cling film and cool completely. Cut into thick slices and serve on a bed of lettuce or watercress with lemon wedges.
Serves 6–8

Prawn and tuna quiche

Metric
For the pastry:
150 g plain flour
1 × 1.25 ml spoon salt
75 g lard and margarine,
    mixed, cut into 1 cm
    cubes
2 × 15 ml spoons cold
    water

For the filling:
150 ml milk
2 eggs
2 large spring onions, cut
    into 2.5 cm lengths
1 × 100 g can tuna,
    drained
6 stuffed green olives
salt
freshly ground black
    pepper
50 g cooked peeled prawns

To garnish:
8 tomato slices
2 stuffed green olives,
    sliced

Imperial
For the pastry:
6 oz plain flour
¼ teaspoon salt
3 oz lard and margarine,
    mixed, cut into ½ inch
    cubes
2 tablespoons cold
    water

For the filling:
¼ pint milk
2 eggs
2 large spring onions, cut
    into 1 inch lengths
1 × 4 oz can tuna,
    drained
6 stuffed green olives
salt
freshly ground black
    pepper
2 oz cooked peeled prawns

To garnish:
8 tomato slices
2 stuffed green olives,
    sliced

Preparation time: about 15 minutes
Cooking time: about 30 minutes
Oven: 200°C, 400°F, Gas Mark 6

To make the pastry, sift the flour and salt into the mixer bowl or large mixing bowl. Add the fat to the flour. Using the mixer, rub the fat into the flour until the mixture resembles fine breadcrumbs. Add the water, using the mixer or by hand, to form a firm dough. Turn out on to a floured surface and knead until smooth. Roll out the dough and use to line a 20 cm/8 inch flan ring or dish.

To make the filling, place all the ingredients, except the prawns, in the blender goblet, with salt and pepper to taste, and blend until the onions and olives are finely chopped. Place the prawns in the pastry case. Pour over the contents of the blender. Arrange the tomato slices around the edge and the olive slices in the centre.

Bake in a preheated oven for 30 minutes or until the pastry is cooked and the filling is set. Serve warm.
Serves 6–8

Variations:
Use canned salmon instead of tuna.
Replace the olives with 2 button mushrooms, sliced.

Pizza fingers

Preparation time: about 30 minutes
Cooking time: about 1 hour
Oven: 200°C, 400°F, Gas Mark 6

Metric	Imperial
For the tomato base:	*For the tomato base:*
1 × 15 ml spoon cooking oil	*1 tablespoon cooking oil*
2 large onions, peeled and roughly chopped	*2 large onions, peeled and roughly chopped*
1 garlic clove, peeled and crushed	*1 garlic clove, peeled and crushed*
1 small green pepper, cored, seeded and roughly chopped	*1 small green pepper, cored, seeded and roughly chopped*
1 × 400 g can tomatoes	*1 × 14 oz can tomatoes*
2 × 15 ml spoons tomato purée	*2 tablespoons tomato purée*
1 small bay leaf	*1 small bay leaf*
1 × 2.5 ml spoon paprika	*½ teaspoon paprika*
salt	*salt*
freshly ground black pepper	*freshly ground black pepper*
For the pizza dough:	*For the pizza dough:*
300 g self-raising flour	*12 oz self-raising flour*
2 × 5 ml spoons salt	*2 teaspoons salt*
75 g margarine	*3 oz margarine*
1 egg	*1 egg*
150 ml milk	*¼ pint milk*
For the topping:	*For the topping:*
3 × 15 ml spoons capers	*3 tablespoons capers*
5 large, or 10 small, salami slices	*5 large, or 10 small, salami slices*
3–4 streaky bacon rashers, rind removed, cut into thin strips lengthways	*3–4 streaky bacon rashers, rind removed, cut into thin strips lengthways*
50 g Cheddar cheese, finely chopped in the blender	*2 oz Cheddar cheese, finely chopped in the blender*
1 × 15 ml spoon cooking oil	*1 tablespoon cooking oil*

To make the tomato base, heat the oil in a medium saucepan, add the onions and garlic and cook gently for 5 minutes. Add all the remaining tomato base ingredients. Bring to the boil, then cover and simmer for 15 minutes.

Remove the lid and cook for a further 10 minutes to reduce the liquid by half. Cool slightly. Discard the bay leaf. Place the tomato mixture in the blender goblet and blend until puréed. Adjust the seasoning. Leave to cool.

To make the pizza dough, sift the flour and salt into the mixer bowl, or a large mixing bowl. Cut the margarine into 1 cm/½ inch cubes and add to the flour. Using the mixer, rub in the margarine until the mixture resembles fine breadcrumbs.

Mix the egg and milk together. If using a table mixer, add the milk mixture to the flour and mix to form a soft dough. Switch off immediately the dough is mixed. If using a hand mixer, mix the milk mixture into the flour with a wooden spoon as this mixture is too stiff for a hand mixer. Turn the dough out on to a floured surface and knead lightly until smooth.

Grease a shallow baking tin, 33 × 23 cm/13 × 9 inches. Roll out the dough to just over the size of the tin, lift into the tin and push the dough well into the sides and corners. Spread the tomato base mixture over the dough. Sprinkle the capers evenly over the top.

Cut large salami slices into four, or small salami slices into halves. Arrange the bacon strips in a lattice design, over the tomato base, with two lines down the length and four lines across the width. Place a piece of salami either side of the lengthways bacon strips and between the crossways strips. Sprinkle the cheese evenly over the top. Dribble on the oil.

Bake in a preheated oven for about 25 minutes or until the dough is golden brown. Serve hot or warm.
Serves 10

Variations:
Use 10 slices of garlic sausage instead of salami.
Use 10 sliced stuffed olives, or stoned black olives, instead of capers.

Prawn and tuna quiche; Pizza fingers

Quick pâté dip

Metric	Imperial
25 g butter	1 oz butter
100 g mushrooms, roughly chopped	4 oz mushrooms, roughly chopped
175 g liver sausage, chopped	6 oz liver sausage, chopped
1 × 5 ml spoon Worcestershire sauce	1 teaspoon Worcestershire sauce
garlic powder	garlic powder
salt	salt
freshly ground black pepper	freshly ground black pepper
1 × 15 ml spoon single or double cream	1 tablespoon single or double cream

Preparation time: 10 minutes
Cooking time: 2 minutes

Melt the butter in a small saucepan, add the mushrooms and cook over a gentle heat for 2 minutes.
Place all the remaining ingredients, except the cream, in the blender goblet, with the garlic powder, and salt and pepper to taste. Add the cooked mushrooms and blend until smooth, scraping down the sides of the goblet, from time to time if necessary. Add the cream and blend until mixed in. Adjust the seasoning, adding extra garlic powder, salt and pepper if required. Turn into a small serving bowl.
Serves 8–10

Cheesy peanut dip

Metric	Imperial
3 × 15 ml spoons salted peanuts	3 tablespoons salted peanuts
175 g mature Cheddar cheese, cut into pieces	6 oz mature Cheddar cheese, cut into pieces
300 ml milk	½ pint milk
25 g butter	1 oz butter
2 × 15 ml spoons plain flour	2 tablespoons plain flour
1 × 5 ml spoon made mustard	1 teaspoon made mustard
2 celery sticks, finely chopped	2 celery sticks, finely chopped
salt	salt
freshly ground black pepper	freshly ground black pepper

Preparation time: 15 minutes
Cooking time: 4 minutes

Chop the peanuts in the blender. Turn out and reserve. Drop the cheese pieces through the centre of the blender lid on to revolving blades to chop finely. Turn out and reserve.
Place the milk, butter, flour and mustard in the blender goblet. Blend for a few seconds or until the flour is mixed in. Pour into a saucepan and bring to the boil, stirring until thickened. Add the cheese and stir until melted. Remove from the heat.
Reserve 2 × 5 ml spoons/2 teaspoons of the chopped peanuts and stir the remaining peanuts and the celery into the cheese sauce. Season well with salt and pepper. Allow to cool, then turn into a serving bowl. Sprinkle over the reserved peanuts before serving.
Serves 8–10 as 1 dip in a selection of 3

Garlic and parsley dip

Metric	Imperial
1 × 425 g can butter beans, drained	1 × 15 oz can butter beans, drained
1 large garlic clove, peeled and crushed or finely chopped	1 large garlic clove, peeled and crushed or finely chopped
1 × 15 ml spoon salad oil	1 tablespoon salad oil
5 × 5 ml spoons lemon juice	5 teaspoons lemon juice
1 × 1.25 ml spoon salt	¼ teaspoon salt
freshly ground black pepper	freshly ground black pepper
3 large parsley sprigs	3 large parsley sprigs

Preparation time: 10 minutes

Place all the ingredients, except the parsley, in the blender goblet. Blend until smooth. It will be necessary to switch off the motor and scrape down the mixture several times. When the mixture is smooth, taste and adjust the seasoning, adding extra lemon juice if necessary. Add the parsley and blend until finely chopped. Turn into a serving bowl.
Serves 8–10 as 1 dip in a selection of 3

From the left: Garlic and parsley dip; Curried mushroom dip; Quick pâté dip; Cheesy peanut dip

Curried mushroom dip

Preparation time: about 10 minutes
Cooking time: 15 minutes

Metric
25 g butter
1 medium onion, peeled
    and roughly chopped
1 × 5 ml spoon curry
    powder
100 g button mushrooms,
    thickly sliced
1 × 1.25 ml spoon salt
freshly ground black
    pepper
100 g cottage cheese
3 × 15 ml spoons soured
    cream
sprig of parsley, to
    garnish (optional)

Imperial
1 oz butter
1 medium onion, peeled
    and roughly chopped
1 teaspoon curry
    powder
4 oz button mushrooms,
    thickly sliced
¼ teaspoon salt
freshly ground black
    pepper
4 oz cottage cheese
3 tablespoons soured
    cream
sprig of parsley, to
    garnish (optional)

Melt the butter in a small pan, add the onion and cook for about 8 minutes over a low heat until soft but not browned. Stir in the curry powder and cook for 2 minutes. Add the mushrooms and cook for 5 minutes. Allow to cool slightly.

Place the mushroom mixture and all the remaining ingredients, except the parsley, in the blender goblet. Blend until very finely chopped. Switch off the motor and scrape down the mixture, if necessary. Taste and adjust the seasoning.

Turn into a serving bowl and garnish with the parsley.
Serves 8–10 as 1 dip in a selection of 3

Chocolate chestnut meringue gâteau

Metric
For the meringue:
4 egg whites
225 g caster sugar

For the chocolate chestnut cream:
1 × 450 g can unsweetened chestnut purée
2 × 15 ml spoons icing sugar, sifted
100 g plain chocolate
2 × 15 ml spoons water
few drops of vanilla essence
2 × 15 ml spoons brandy or rum
150 ml double or whipping cream

To decorate:
150 ml double or whipping cream
25 g plain chocolate

Imperial
For the meringue:
4 egg whites
8 oz caster sugar

For the chocolate chestnut cream:
1 × 16 oz can unsweetened chestnut purée
2 tablespoons icing sugar, sifted
4 oz plain chocolate
2 tablespoons water
few drops of vanilla essence
2 tablespoons brandy or rum
¼ pint double or whipping cream

To decorate:
¼ pint double or whipping cream
1 oz plain chocolate

Preparation time: about 45 minutes (excluding overnight storage time)
Cooking time: about 1 hour
Oven: 120°C, 250°F, Gas Mark ½

To make the meringue, place the egg whites in the mixer bowl or a large mixing bowl. Using the mixer, whisk the whites on a high speed until very stiff. They should stand in stiff peaks when the beaters are lifted out of the bowl and look dull rather than shiny. Add half of the sugar and whisk until very stiff and shiny. Using a low speed, fold in the remaining sugar.

Cover baking sheets with non-stick baking paper. Spread or pipe the meringue mixture into 3 × 20 cm/ 8 inch diameter rounds. Bake in a preheated oven for about 1 hour or until crisp and dried out. Cool.

To make the chestnut cream, place the chestnut purée in the mixer bowl or a large mixing bowl. Using the mixer, beat the chestnut purée to break it up. Add the sugar and beat until smooth. Place the chocolate and water in a small heatproof basin over a pan of simmering water to melt. Beat the melted chocolate into the chestnut purée with vanilla essence and brandy or rum. Place the cream in a medium bowl and whip until just stiff, using a hand mixer or whisk. Add the cream to the chestnut mixture and mix together using a low speed on the mixer.

To make up, spread 2 meringue rounds with the chestnut mixture, using about one-quarter of the mixture. Place one of the rounds on a flat serving plate. Top with the other round. Place the remaining meringue round on top. Spread the remaining chestnut mixture over the top and sides to cover completely. Cover loosely with foil or with a polythene container and store in the refrigerator overnight.

The next day, to decorate, place the cream in the mixer bowl or a medium mixing bowl. Using the mixer whip until just thick and of a piping consistency. Place in a piping bag fitted with a star nozzle. Pipe the cream around the top edge of the gâteau. Break the chocolate into pieces and drop through the centre of the blender lid on to revolving blades to chop it. Alternatively, grate the chocolate using a coarse grater. Sprinkle the chocolate over the gâteau.
Serves 12

Nutty meringue with peaches

Metric	**Imperial**
50 g blanched almonds	2 oz blanched almonds
50 g walnut pieces	2 oz walnut pieces
1 × 2.5 ml spoon mixed spice	½ teaspoon mixed spice
4 egg whites	4 egg whites
225 g caster sugar	8 oz caster sugar

For the filling:

150 ml double or whipping cream	¼ pint double or whipping cream
1 × 225 g can sliced peaches, drained and coarsely chopped	1 × 8 oz can sliced peaches, drained and coarsely chopped
50 g green grapes, halved and pips removed	2 oz green grapes, halved and pips removed

Preparation time: about 25 minutes
Cooking time: 35–40 minutes
Oven: 190°C, 375°F, Gas Mark 5

Butter the sides and bottom of two 20 cm/8 inch sandwich tins, and flour the sides. Line the bottom of each tin with a disc of non-stick silicone paper.

Toast the almonds under a moderate grill until golden. Cool. Chop finely in the blender by dropping through the centre of the blender lid on to revolving blades. Turn out into a bowl. Likewise, chop the walnuts, and add to the almonds with the mixed spice. Place the egg whites in the mixer bowl or large mixing bowl. Using the mixer, whisk the whites on a high speed until very stiff. They should stand in stiff peaks when the beaters are lifted from the mixture and look dull rather than shiny. Gradually add the sugar, whisking well between each addition. When all the sugar has been added the whites should be very stiff and shiny. Using a metal spoon, fold in the nut mixture. Divide between the prepared tins and spread evenly with a palette knife.

Bake in a preheated oven for 35–40 minutes, until the outside is crisp and just beginning to brown. The centre should be slightly moist. Loosen the edges with a palette knife and leave for about 5 minutes. Turn out carefully on to a wire tray and cool.

To make the filling, place the cream in the mixer bowl, or medium mixing bowl. Using the mixer, whisk the cream until just stiff, then reserve about one-third. Spread the remaining cream over one meringue round and scatter chopped peaches on top. Reserve 8 grape halves and arrange the remaining grapes between the peaches. Cover with the second meringue round and decorate the top with cream and grapes. Serves 8

From the left: Nutty meringue with peaches; Chocolate chestnut meringue gâteau

Cherry Pavlova

Metric
3 egg whites
175 g caster sugar
few drops vanilla essence
1 × 2.5 ml spoon lemon
   juice
1 × 2.5 spoon cornflour

For the filling:
150 ml double or
   whipping cream
1 × 425 g can stoned
   black cherries
2 × 5 ml spoons arrowroot

Imperial
3 egg whites
6 oz caster sugar
few drops vanilla essence
½ teaspoon lemon
   juice
½ teaspoon cornflour

For the filling:
¼ pint double or
   whipping cream
1 × 15 oz can stoned
   black cherries
2 teaspoons arrowroot

Preparation time: about 15 minutes
Cooking time: about 1 hour
Oven: 150°C, 300°F, Gas Mark 2
Cover a baking sheet with non-stick silicone paper and draw a 23 cm/9 inch circle.
Place the egg whites in the mixer bowl, or a large mixing bowl. Using the mixer, whisk the whites on a high speed until very stiff. They should stand in straight peaks when the beaters are lifted from the mixture and look dull rather than shiny. Add the sugar gradually, whisking well between each addition to keep the whites very stiff. When all the sugar has been added the whites should be very stiff and look shiny. Add the vanilla essence and lemon juice. Using a low speed fold in the cornflour.
Place about half of the mixture in a piping bag fitted with a large star nozzle. Spread the remaining mixture into the marked circle on the paper, making the edge slightly thicker than the centre. Pipe swirls of the mixture, almost touching, around the edge. Place in a preheated oven for about 1 hour, until pale gold brown. The meringue should be crisp on the outside and slightly moist inside. Leave to cool on the paper, then transfer carefully to a serving plate.
To make the filling, place the cream in the mixer bowl or a medium mixing bowl. Using the mixer whisk the cream until just thick. Spread over the meringue.
Drain the cherry juice into a small pan. Blend the arrowroot with 2 × 15 ml spoons/2 tablespoons of the juice. Bring the remaining juice to the boil, stir in the arrowroot mixture and cook, stirring, until thickened. Cool. Arrange the cherries on the cream and spoon the thickened juice over to glaze.
Serves 6–8

Mocha choux ring

Metric
For the pastry:
65 g plain flour
pinch of salt
50 g butter
150 ml water
2 eggs, beaten
25 g blanched almonds,
  chopped in the blender

For the filling:
1 × 15 ml spoon custard
  powder
2 × 5 ml spoons instant
  coffee powder
150 ml plus 2 × 15 ml
  spoons milk
1 × 15 ml spoon sugar
150 ml double cream

To serve:
double quantity Dark
  Chocolate Sauce
  (page 43)
2 × 15 ml spoons brandy
  or rum
sifted icing sugar

Imperial
For the pastry:
2½ oz plain flour
pinch of salt
2 oz butter
¼ pint water
2 eggs, beaten
1 oz blanched almonds,
  chopped in the blender

For the filling:
1 tablespoon custard
  powder
2 teaspoons instant
  coffee powder
¼ pint plus 2 tablespoons
  milk
1 tablespoon sugar
¼ pint double cream

To serve:
double quantity Dark
  Chocolate Sauce
  (page 43)
2 tablespoons brandy
  or rum
sifted icing sugar

Preparation time: about 35 minutes
Cooking time: about 30 minutes
Oven: 200°C, 400°F, Gas Mark 6

To make the choux pastry, sift the flour and salt together. Place the butter and water in a medium saucepan, heat to melt the butter and bring to the boil. Remove from the heat, add the flour and beat until the mixture forms a soft ball and leaves the sides of the pan. Turn into the mixer bowl, or a medium mixing bowl. Using the mixer, gradually add the beaten eggs beating after each addition for about 20 seconds. Make about six additions in all. The mixture should be smooth, glossy and of piping consistency.

Place the mixture in a large piping bag fitted with a plain 1 cm/½ inch nozzle. Pipe rounds, 4 cm/1½ inches in diameter and about 1 cm/½ inch apart, on a greased baking sheet to form a 20 cm/8 inch diameter circle. Sprinkle the almonds over the top. Bake in a pre-heated oven for about 30 minutes or until well-risen, golden and crisp. Cool on a wire tray.

To make the filling, blend the custard powder and instant coffee with the 2 × 15 ml spoons/2 tablespoons of milk. Bring the 150 ml/¼ pint of milk to the boil in a saucepan and pour on to the custard mixture, stirring. Return to the pan, add the sugar and cook, stirring, until thickened. Cover with cling film and cool.

Place the cream in the mixer bowl, or a medium mixing bowl. Using the mixer, whip the cream until just thick. If using a table mixer, transfer the cream to a small bowl. Place the custard in the mixer bowl and whisk until smooth. Using a low speed mix the cream and custard together and switch off immediately the mixture is combined.

If using a hand mixer, place the custard in a medium bowl and whisk until smooth. Using the lowest speed mix the cream and custard and switch off immediately the mixture is combined.

Prepare the chocolate sauce, add the brandy or rum and cool.

To serve, split the choux ring in half, spread the coffee filling thickly over the bottom half of the ring, and cover with the top half. Dust with icing sugar. Serve the chocolate sauce separately.
Serves 8

Variations:
Use 300 ml/½ pint whipped cream only for the filling and flavour with a few drops of vanilla essence.
Omit the instant coffee and add 1 × 400 g/14 oz can pears, drained and chopped, to the filling.

From the left: Mocha choux ring; Cherry Pavlova

Index